"We live in an age that has a woeful lack of honor and respect in the home, the state, and the church. Children dishonor their parents, citizens dishonor their civil leaders, and church members often dishonor their pastors. All this is rooted in a lack of proper honor for God, who is sovereign over the spheres of the home, the state, and the church. In his excellent book *The Honor of God*, Grant Castleberry drives home the importance of restoring a proper honor for God that will have a generational impact on the whole of life."

—Dr. Josh Buice
Pastor, Pray's Mill Baptist Church
Founder and President, G3 Ministries

"At the heart of every culture are certain key values that shape and determine life and thought within that culture. The modern West has a number of such values, but honor and shame are not among them. For Christians, this is particularly challenging, since the world of the Bible is one in which honor and glory, on the one hand, and shame and disgrace, on the other, are major determinants of life. This new work by Pastor Castleberry is, therefore, most welcome, as it helps to reorient our living and thinking around this biblical axis of honor and shame."

—Dr. Michael A.G. Haykin
Professor of Church History
The Southern Baptist Theological Seminary, Louisville, Ky.

"As Western society has progressed (or regressed) over the last many years, we have largely lost the notions of honor and shame. More than simply ethical or cultural, these are certainly biblical. And I can think of no one more qualified to write about them than Grant Castleberry. In *The Honor of God*, Grant aptly explores the weightiness of God's glory and the shamefulness of sin, propelling the reader to consider the ramifications of reclaiming the biblical view of both. He contends that we are to elevate our view of God's transcendent majesty and give Him all the honor and glory due His name. This book will challenge you, convict you, and captivate you."

—Dr. Nate Pickowicz
Pastor, Harvest Bible Church
Gilmanton Iron Works, N.H.

The Honor of God

The Honor of God

GRANT R. CASTLEBERRY

LIGONIER MINISTRIES

The Honor of God
© 2025 by Grant R. Castleberry

Published by Ligonier Ministries
421 Ligonier Court, Sanford, FL 32771
Ligonier.org

Printed in York, Pennsylvania
Maple Press
0000125
First printing

ISBN 978-1-64289-633-6 (Hardcover)
ISBN 978-1-64289-634-3 (ePub)

Cover design: Lydia Cockrell
Interior design and typeset: Katherine Lloyd, The DESK

Library of Congress Control Number: 2024931284

To my wife and co-laborer in the gospel,

GraceAnna Castleberry

"An excellent wife who can find?

She is far more precious than jewels."

Proverbs 31:10

And to our children:

AudreyKate, Evangeline, Charles, Patrick, and Truman.

May you each live for God's honor

all the days of your lives.

Contents

PART ONE

Introduction

The honor of God lies at the fabric of our existence. This is because the honor of God is the chief end of God. God created the universe and everything in it for this one ultimate purpose: *the honor of His own name.*

This momentous realization came to me when I was a young man, and in some ways, it has possessed me ever since. It is one of those great themes that once you understand it, you can never forget it. For the past twenty years, I have studied this theme as it unfolds across the Bible, and it has transformed the way I think about God and myself. It is no overstatement to say that the *honor of God* has become one of the defining themes of my life and the foundation of my worldview.

I also believe that it is one of the key elements in recovering biblical Christianity. The basic meaning of *honor* is "weightiness." Honoring God means that we view His character, His rule, and His sovereignty as the *weightiest* realities in our lives. Unfortunately, this aspect of God's weightiness is largely missing in modern Christianity, where it has been lost amid a wave of frivolous worship that puts man at the center. In many worship services, Christians are exposed to a version of God who is not God at all.

Instead, they encounter a version of God who is an encouraging life coach who simply wants us to be the best version of ourselves.

But that is not the God of the Bible. The God of the Bible is the Lord of the cosmos, the "judge of the living and the dead" (Acts 10:42), and the loving Savior of the world (John 3:16). The God of the Bible is, in a word, *holy.*

God is truly awesome—death-defyingly awesome. Yet in Christ, we fear Him not as sinners who will be judged but as sons of our kind heavenly Father who reigns over heaven and earth. There is a reason that Solomon declared, "The fear of the LORD is the beginning of wisdom, and the knowledge of the Holy One is insight" (Prov. 9:10). The God-centered life emerges when we see God as He really is.

The Loss of Honor

To compound the issue, many moderns have lost the lens through which to see and understand God in the way that He is presented in the Bible. This is because we lack a framework for the concepts of *honor* and *shame.* In our modern world, wealth often takes precedence over honor. Many people would rather be wealthy, indeed infamous—even for doing something shameful—than preserve their own honor. What matters more in many people's minds is popularity and wealth, even if that popularity comes at the expense of their honor.

This reality of the loss of honor was pressed home to me when I was series commander at Marine Corps Recruit Depot Parris Island. One of my jobs was to teach the recruits the core values of the United States Marine Corps. To do this, I gathered three to four hundred recruits in a large auditorium, and I taught them the Marines' core values of *honor*, *courage*, and *commitment*, which have been the core values of the Marine Corps since 1775.

The recruits understood *courage* quite easily. Courage is acting in the presence of danger despite our fear. It is being able to move forward and act with bravery in the face of danger. They also understood *commitment*, which means being "all in" and giving it our all, even when there is great cost in achieving the goal. But the value that they struggled to understand was *honor*. I began to teach them the concept by having them stand and sing the Marine Corps hymn at attention. I did this because there is a section of the hymn that goes:

> First to fight for right and freedom
> And to keep our honor clean;
> We are proud to claim the title
> Of United States Marine.

I explained to them what the line "to keep our honor clean" means by telling them how the Marine Corps had carried a certain weightiness in history. People respected Marines because they have fought and won some of America's toughest battles. Keeping the honor clean, then, means not doing anything to compromise that respect. I emphasized that it means a great deal to pin that eagle, globe, and anchor on the collar of one's uniform and that every Marine has a responsibility to bring honor to the corps, our nation, and our fellow Marines. To bring shame through our actions would be a catastrophic failure for a Marine. When the Marine Corps is brought up in conversation, we want people to respect and speak highly of the corps.

Often, even after this hymn exercise, I was still met with confused faces. Honor was simply a difficult concept to grasp for eighteen- and nineteen-year-old recruits who had grown up in secularist America, so I explained it with examples of famous Marines such as Chesty Puller, John Basilone, and Alexander Bonnyman, who had brought honor to corps and country by serving with distinction. These examples brought a sense of dignity and renown to the Marine Corps that should not be tarnished by other Marines. Finally, the message began to break through to the recruits. Honor is simply a foreign idea in our modern culture.

Defining *Honor*

Remember the names Aaron Burr and Alexander Hamilton? Besides their pivotal role in early American politics, they are famous for taking part in a tragic duel against each other. A duel seems like a foreign contest to us moderns because we often fail to understand the element that lies at its heart—*honor*. A duel took place when someone's honor had been slighted. In the case of Burr and Hamilton, Hamilton had slighted Burr's character when he had opposed Burr and instead favored his archrival Thomas Jefferson in the election for vice president.[1] In Burr's mind, his honor demanded vindication, so Burr challenged Hamilton to a duel, which Burr subsequently won. Hamilton died a day later.

I often wear a pair of old Allen Edmonds dress shoes. I try to keep them shined up as best as I can because they belonged to my grandfather. To honor him, I often wear these shoes when I preach on Sunday mornings. They remind me visually of the weightiness of his influence on my life. Every day, we do all sorts of things like this that demonstrate honor. When we stand up for the Pledge of

Allegiance or the national anthem and put our right hand over our heart, we demonstrate honor. We are making a public display that our nation weighs "heavy" in our lives.

How does the Bible define honor? The Hebrew word used to translate "honor" is *kabod*, which literally means being "weighty," "heavy," or "severe." Sometimes it is translated in the Old Testament as "glory." The basic idea is that honoring something or someone means that we are showing the heaviness or weightiness of that person in our life. In the New Testament, the Greek verbs *timaō* and *megalynō* basically mean the same thing—that we are giving honor or deference, showing the heaviness of something, respecting something, or showing admiration for something. On the flip side is the concept of *shame*. To shame something is to treat it as though it were nothing.

The World of the Bible

The concepts of honor and shame were foundational to the worldview of the biblical authors. They were also foundational in how God dealt with the nation of Israel in the Old Testament and with the church in the New Testament. The fifth commandment states, "Honor your father and your mother, that your days may be long in the land that the LORD your God is giving you" (Ex. 20:12). Children have a responsibility to God to honor their parents. This means that they are to respect their parents as "weighty" in their lives.

Similarly, David prays in Psalm 31:1, "In you, O LORD, do I take refuge; let me never be put to shame; in your righteousness deliver me!" A few verses later, in verse 11, David laments, "Because of all my adversaries I have become a reproach, especially to my neighbors, and an object of dread to my acquaintances; those who see me in the street flee from me." It is this idea of being treated lightly that he dreads. In his mind, one of the most fearful realities was that the people of Israel would shame him.

In Psalm 35:26, David prays this for his enemies: "Let them be put to shame and disappointed altogether who rejoice at my calamity! Let them be clothed with shame and dishonor who magnify themselves against me!" With the exception of their death in final judgment, this was the worst thing that one could pray against others. David is saying, essentially: "Let them be clothed with shame. Let my enemies be treated with contempt."

In reference to all the horrific things that the Babylonians did to Israel, the prophet Jeremiah said, "We are put to shame, for we have heard reproach; dishonor has covered our face, for foreigners have come into the holy places of the LORD's house" (Jer. 51:51). Jeremiah interpreted the Babylonians' coming into the temple in terms of shame and reproach on the people. In another example, when the opponents of the Jews tried to stop the building of the second temple, they wrote to King Artaxerxes, "Now because we eat the salt of the palace and it is not fitting for us to witness the king's dishonor, therefore we send and inform the king" (Ezra 4:14). They invoked the king's honor to try to impede the construction of the temple.

The opening pages of the New Testament demonstrate that the world at that time was still very much an honor/shame world. After Joseph found out that Mary was pregnant, he decided to "divorce her quietly" because he was "a just man and unwilling to put her to shame" (Matt. 1:19). Joseph knew that if he divorced Mary, her life would be marked by shame.

In one of the most famous verses of the New Testament, Paul declared in Romans 1:16, "For I am not ashamed of the gospel." Everywhere in the ancient world, when the gospel was preached, it conveyed shame to many listeners because it was the message of a crucified Savior. In the ancient world, there was no greater picture of shame than someone's dying naked on a cross. Paul stated in 1 Corinthians 1:23 that the cross was folly to gentiles and foolishness to Jews because they understood the cross to be a place of cursing. Therefore, the message was considered shameful. Yet Paul boasted, "I am not ashamed of the gospel." He would not allow himself to be ashamed because he had seen its power unleashed in people's lives: "It is the power of God for salvation" (Rom. 1:16).

Paul was also concerned that the evangelists who worked with him not bring unnecessary reproach and shame to the gospel. Paul told Timothy, "Do your best to present yourself to God as one approved, a worker who has no need to be ashamed, rightly handling the word of truth" (2 Tim. 2:15). Why might Timothy be ashamed? First, if he disqualified himself morally by committing a grievous sin that brought reproach on the name of Christ. Second, if he failed in his duties to properly teach the Word of God. Therefore, Paul essentially says to Timothy, "Rightly handle the word of truth so that you do not bring reproach and shame on the office of pastor."

Similarly, he told Timothy in 1 Timothy 6:13–14, "I charge you in the presence of God, who gives life to all things, and of Christ Jesus, who in his testimony before Pontius Pilate made the good confession, to keep the commandment unstained and free from reproach." Reproach is shame. Timothy was instructed to keep the commands and teachings of Christ and the Apostles "free from reproach" until Christ returned. To Titus, Paul pointed out that good character brings shame to one's opponents: "Show yourself in all respects to be a model of good works, and in your teaching show integrity, dignity, and sound speech that cannot be condemned, so that an opponent may be put to shame, having nothing evil to say about us" (Titus 2:7–8).

Not only were saints exhorted to bring honor to the gospel, but they were implored to give honor to God. Paul made the remarkable statement to Timothy that God "alone has immortality, who dwells in unapproachable light, whom no one has ever seen or can see. To him be honor and eternal dominion. Amen" (1 Tim. 6:16). As we realize God's transcendent character, our only proper response is to give Him honor. This is the vertical aspect of honor in the Christian life.

Paul was stressing that the defining reality in our lives should be the weightiness of God. He was saying that God is to press on us in such a way that we live our lives to honor Him. This should be the driving impulse in the church as well—that in everything the name of God would be honored and that our lives would not bring Him reproach.

Recovering Biblical Christianity

Unfortunately, this concern for God's honor and reverence for His holiness has disappeared like a mist on a hot day. It has been replaced with a watered-down understanding of both God and the gospel. This is reflected in the aesthetics, the music, the posture, and most of all the preaching of the modern church. Much preaching has been reduced to a mixture of comedy and pragmatism:

"How can you be a better parent? How can you be a better steward of your finances?" Even pulpits have been traded in for tables littered with trinkets. Everything is casual, with one of the main goals being that no one would ever feel uncomfortable.

What is missing? It is the *vision of a holy God*. It is the authority of God's Word. It is the reverence for His character. I believe that the state of the church is so dismal because God is simply not seen in much of evangelical worship. How can we see God if we do not open and deeply study His Word? In short, how can we live a reverent life if we have never encountered God?

I once saw a documentary about climbers who set out to climb K2, the second-highest mountain in the world. Many say that it is the hardest mountain in the world to climb. In the documentary, the cameraman is walking behind the climbers as they make their way to K2 base camp, from which they will begin their ascent of the mountain. In perhaps the most dramatic part of the documentary, they round a curve in the trail and catch a glimpse of K2 for the first time. When they see it, fear rushes over them. They are blown away in sheer terror at the size of the mountain.[2] It is one thing to know that K2 is the second-tallest mountain; it is quite another to stand before its face. I have noticed the same thing when people truly encounter God. There is an awe factor. There is shock and amazement. There is quietness after the service ends. I believe that this is how it should be. Furthermore, there are three fundamental realizations when you encounter God: (1) that God is holy, (2) that you are a great sinner, and (3) that His Word is true. You are left with the impression that these are the most true realities in the universe. It is from this mindset that God calls us to live before Him.

An important Latin phrase that came out of the Reformation fleshes out this idea: *coram Deo*, which means "before the face of God." I was first exposed to this idea while listening to R.C. Sproul's lectures on *The Holiness of God*.[3] I was struck by the truth that the reality of God is to press down on us so that everything is different. Our ethics, our morals, our family life, our work, and our worship are all transformed underneath the all-encompassing shadow of a holy God. We are to live *coram Deo*—before the face of God. This is the essence of a biblical worldview. We view all of life in the light of its Creator. We live for His honor.

The Weightiness of God

The writer of Hebrews says, "Therefore let us be grateful for receiving a kingdom that cannot be shaken, and thus let us offer to God acceptable worship, with reverence and awe, for our God is a consuming fire" (Heb. 12:28–29). The Greek word used for "reverence" is *eulabeia*. It means "reverent awe in the presence of God" and is used to describe the holy fear of God. The writer of Hebrews emphasizes that this reverence should define our worship of God, even as new covenant believers.

The author uses this word one other time, in Hebrews 5:7. It is a startling appearance of the word because he uses it to describe the actions of the Lord Jesus Christ: "In the days of his flesh, Jesus offered up prayers and supplications, with loud cries and tears, to him who was able to save him from death, and he was heard because of his *reverence*"—because of His *eulabeia*. Jesus Christ is the eternal Son of God. He was with God the Father from all eternity. He and the Father are one: "In the beginning was the Word, and the Word was with God, and the Word was God" (John 1:1).

Yet the writer of Hebrews says that throughout His ministry, Jesus approached the Father with "reverence." His *reverence for God* defined His interactions with the Father. He was heard because of His holy awe for God. This gives us great insight into how the Lord Jesus lived His life. He lived *coram Deo*—with a huge vision of God. He never lost that vision of God. It never slipped from view, and no obstacle ever eclipsed it. No Pharisee or Sadducee ever impeded it. The devil himself could not diminish it. The vision of God consumed Jesus.

God as a "Consuming Fire"

If this is how the Lord Jesus approached the Father, we too must approach God with this type of reverence and awe (Heb. 12:28). "Awe" means that we tremble at the awesomeness of God. We use the word *awesome* all the time, but it really should be reserved for what is most awesome—namely, God—because "our God is a consuming fire" (v. 29). When was the last time you heard God described as a "consuming fire" in a sermon or in a discipleship meeting? We are so used to focusing on the immanent God who comforts us that we tend to forget His transcendence and holiness. He is outside space and time. He is holy, omnipotent, eternal, righteous, and all-powerful. He is a "consuming fire."

Perhaps the writer of Hebrews was thinking about the manifestation of God to Moses on the great mountain of God, Mount Sinai. According to Exodus 24:12–13: "The LORD said to Moses, 'Come up to me on the mountain and wait there, that I may give you the tablets of stone, with the law and the commandment, which I have written for their instruction.' So Moses rose with his assistant Joshua, and Moses went up into the mountain of God."

The rest of the children of Israel were not allowed to go up on the mountain. They had pylons around the entire mountain that were basically "Do Not Enter" signs. The elders were allowed to come up to a certain point, but even they were not allowed to go up the mountain. If anyone transgressed these boundary markers, he would be struck dead by God.

The text says: "Then Moses went up on the mountain, and the cloud covered the mountain. The glory [the *kabod*] of the LORD dwelt on Mount Sinai" (vv. 15–16). Literally, the heavy presence of God dwelt on the mountain. This glory was so transcendent and so holy that it is hard to even picture what it must have looked like. "And the cloud covered it six days. And on the seventh day he called to Moses out of the midst of the cloud" (v. 16). Then the text says, "Now the appearance of the glory of the LORD was like a devouring fire" (v. 17).

The manifestation of God was a consuming fire—scorching the top of the mountain. Remarkably, Moses went into that cloud of fire for forty days and forty nights. That picture of God is what the writer of Hebrews is wanting us to think about—this awesome encounter with a holy God. For this reason, we approach God through our Great High Priest, the Lord Jesus Christ. But we still approach Him with reverence and awe.

I once heard theologian Sinclair Ferguson speak about an event that occurred in his life when he was a young man. Dr. D. Martyn Lloyd-Jones came to Scotland to preach when Ferguson was a teenager.[4] The first night that Lloyd-Jones preached, Ferguson could not attend. The next day, he spoke to a friend who had gone to hear him. He asked her something along these lines: "What was it like to hear Dr. Lloyd-Jones preach?"

She looked at him quietly and then said, "It felt like the building was about to fall down."

The presence of God had been so tangibly felt that it seemed like the walls of the building were going to collapse. That is reverent Christianity. It is a genuine encounter with God through His Word that changes us. We feel His presence pressing on us through His Word in a demonstrable way. Paul called it a "demonstration of the Spirit and of power" (1 Cor. 2:4). Until we recover that, we have not recovered truly reverent Christianity. True Christianity is knowing God. It is living *coram Deo*. It is reverence and awe for God.

Lloyd-Jones once said, "True Christianity is the recovery of the awareness of the awesomeness of God."[5] He went on to say: "The basis of everything is the sovereign, transcendent, living God, who in his eternal, glorious freedom, acts, intervenes, and interferes with the life of the whole Church and of individuals. And if there is anything that is more obvious than anything else in the life of the Church today, it is the failure to start with, and to believe, that truth."[6]

This is the problem of the modern church. We have not started with the reality of the transcendent God. Without this understanding, it is impossible to comprehend the problem of sin as it relates to God. And without a proper understanding of the problem of sin, we cannot understand the real meaning of the atonement. A substitutionary atonement makes sense only in the light of a holy God. We cannot explain the reality of sin without the reality of a holy God. Everything hinges on understanding the reality of a transcendent God.

Lloyd-Jones said this back in 1959, and today, we see the negligible effect that Christianity is having on Western culture. The church became impotent when it put man in the place of God. If God is not a heavy reality in the churches, why should He be a heavy reality in the world? God does not call us to comfortableness. In fact, the vision of God as a "consuming fire" is very uncomfortable. But it is this vision that will inspire us to sanctification. The Apostle Peter reminds us that it is written, "You shall be holy, for I am holy" (1 Peter 1:16).

In other words, God's holiness is to drive us to holiness. I remember once going to a movie with my grandfather, and he walked out fifteen minutes after the movie started because God's name was blasphemed. For him, that was worse than anything else. He carried with him a sense of the Lord's holiness. If we are going to recover this vision of God, we must recover this sense of reverence for God. We should shudder when God's name is shamed and dishonored.

If the modern church would recover this type of reverence for God, I believe that churches would fill up again. People would drive from far and wide to encounter the living God. The world would have to stop and take notice of the phenomenon of Christianity because of the reality of God in our lives. It all begins with the reality of being God-centered people who know His weightiness in our own personal lives.

1

The Rule of Honor

First Samuel 2:30 introduces us to what I call the *rule of honor*: "Therefore the LORD, the God of Israel, declares: 'I promised that your house and the house of your father should go in and out before me forever,' but now the LORD declares: 'Far be it from me, for those who honor me I will honor, and those who despise me shall be lightly esteemed.'" This rule of honor always holds true.

I was first exposed to this rule as a boy. My mom rented a movie called *Chariots of Fire*, which is based on the true story of two British runners named Eric Liddell and Harold Abrahams. Viewers soon realize that Liddell is motivated by something very different from what motivates the other runners. He is motivated by the *honor of God*, to advance the fame of God's name. At one point in the film, Liddell remarks: "To run and to win is to honor Him. And when I run, I feel His pleasure."

These words were not mere lip service. Before the 1924 Olympic Games, Liddell learned that the qualifying heats for the 100-meter dash would be held on a Sunday. He told the British Olympic Committee that he could not run on a Sunday because it would dishonor

God by breaking the fourth commandment. They pressured Liddell to run, but he would not relent. Finally, the committee decided that he would run the 400-meter dash instead of the 100-meter. The 400-meter dash, which equals one lap around the track, is known for the tough demands it places on the runner.

Liddell ran an astonishing race that summer in Paris and won Olympic gold, setting a world record in the process.[1] It was a remarkable accomplishment. The second-place finisher, American Horatio Fitch, said after the race: "I had no idea he would win it. I couldn't believe a man could set such a pace and finish."[2]

In the film, an American runner who had heard about Liddell's decision to not run on Sunday approached Liddell before his race and handed him a note containing a portion of 1 Samuel 2:30, "He who honors me, I will honor." In real life, it was a trainer who had given Liddell the note. And this note, which served as an inspiration to Liddell, stated this nonnegotiable rule of honor.

To better understand this rule of honor, it's vital to understand the context of this verse. As the book of 1 Samuel opens, Eli is the priest of Israel. His sons, who serve as priests alongside him, have dishonored the Lord by eating the choice meats that were to be given to God in the sacrifices. Eli's sons were also fornicating with prostitutes at the front of the tabernacle of the Lord. An unnamed "man of God" comes to Eli, pronouncing God's judgment on Eli and on the priesthood of the line of Aaron. The indictment of the prophet is that Eli has treated his sons as weightier than the Lord. Then this man of God communicates the rule of honor: "Therefore the LORD, the God of Israel, declares: 'I promised that your house and the house of your father should go in and out before me forever,' but now the LORD declares: 'Far be it from me, for those who honor me I will honor, and those who despise me shall be lightly esteemed'" (1 Sam. 2:30).

Notice what the man of God says. God will honor those who honor Him. God will treat as weighty those who treat God as weighty. The reverse is true as well. God will lightly esteem those who despise Him. Eli and his sons would be judged because they had treated God flippantly. This is the rule of honor. If we honor God, God will honor us. If we shame God, God will shame us.

The Rule of Honor in Scripture

Once we understand this rule, we begin to see it throughout Scripture. For example, David teaches this principle in Psalm 37:39–40:

> The salvation of the righteous is from the LORD;
>> he is their stronghold in the time of trouble.
> The LORD helps them and delivers them;
>> he delivers them from the wicked and saves them,
> because they take refuge in him.

David is confident of the Lord's deliverance because he is honoring the Lord by taking refuge in Him. The Psalms are replete with similar statements.

God declares through Hosea 10:12:

> Sow for yourselves righteousness;
>> reap steadfast love;
>> break up your fallow ground,
> for it is the time to seek the LORD,
>> that he may come and rain righteousness upon you.

The prophet says that the Lord rains righteousness on those who seek Him. Those who honor the Lord, the Lord honors.

We see the opposite reality in the book of Daniel. On the evening that Babylon falls to invaders, Nebuchadnezzar's son Belshazzar sees a hand writing on the wall. No one is able to understand the script, so Daniel is called in to interpret. Daniel says to Belshazzar, "You have praised the gods of silver and gold, of bronze, iron, wood, and stone, which do not see or hear or know, but the God in whose hand is your breath, and whose are all your ways, you have not honored" (Dan. 5:23). Daniel goes on to give a message of judgment. As a result, that very night Belshazzar and his forces are wiped out by the Medes and the Persians.

In Malachi 2:1–2, after Judah has returned from exile, Malachi declares: "And now, O priests, this command is for you. If you will not listen, if you will not take it to heart to give honor to my name, says the LORD of hosts, then I will send the curse upon you and I will curse your blessings." In other words, Malachi restates the rule of honor.

These examples from the Old Testament might cause us to ask if God still operates this way in the New Testament. We see Jesus say in John 12:26, "If anyone serves me, the Father will honor him." By this, Jesus means that believers who honor Christ now will receive much honor in His eternal kingdom. In Romans 1:21, the Apostle Paul states, "For although they knew God, they did not honor him as God or give thanks to him, but they became futile in their thinking, and their foolish hearts were darkened."

We see here the rule of honor. If an individual fails to give honor to God after seeing His wonderful works in creation, God hands that person over to judgment. In other words, God treats the person lightly. Paul warns that those who do not honor God become "futile in their thinking" and their "foolish hearts" are "darkened" (Rom. 1:21). We are seeing this reality on display in our modern world. A culture that fails to honor God will be given over to shame and reproach by God, and that is precisely what is happening. If we fail to honor God, if we esteem God lightly, God will treat us lightly. This is the rule of honor.

A Case Study in the Rule of Honor

First Samuel 17 provides us with a case study in what it means to honor God. The honor of God is the theme of David's encounter with the Philistine giant Goliath. Verse 1 opens, "Now the Philistines gathered their armies for battle. And they were gathered at Socoh, which belongs to Judah." The Philistines, who worshiped the false god Dagon, were a seafaring people who lived on the Mediterranean coast southwest of Israel. They were not a unified nation; rather, they consisted of five city-states. Gath, where Goliath was from, was one of those city-states. Renowned for their iron weaponry, the Philistines often possessed a great advantage over the Israelites. They were fierce warriors who sadistically tortured their prisoners. Verse 1 contains a detail that would have stood out to its Jewish listeners: the Philistines go to "Socoh, which belongs to Judah." This is the land that God promised through covenant to Israel in Genesis 12 and Genesis 15. Socoh, where the Philistines have gone, is part of the promised land that God gave to Israel.

The narrative continues: "And Saul and the men of Israel were gathered, and encamped in the Valley of Elah, and drew up in line of battle against the Philistines. And the Philistines stood on the mountain on the one side, and Israel stood on the mountain on the other side, with a valley between them. And there came out from the camp of the Philistines a champion named Goliath of Gath, whose height was six cubits and a span" (1 Sam. 17:2–4). As a boy, I loved watching basketball player Shaquille O'Neal. O'Neal stood at over seven feet tall and weighed more than three hundred pounds. Moreover, he possessed exceptional quickness and stamina for a man of his size. But Goliath was approximately nine feet tall, roughly two feet taller than Shaq! That is a mind-boggling picture. The Hebrew word for "champion" literally means "middleman." A middleman would go and fight between the lines. Sometimes armies would settle their differences by sending out champions to fight against one another, rather than sacrificing their entire armies. Goliath was the Philistine middleman, a "champion."

He must have been incredibly strong, for "he had a helmet of bronze on his head, and he was armed with a coat of mail, and the weight of the coat was five thousand shekels of bronze" (1 Sam. 17:5). That is roughly 125 to 150 pounds of armor. Even the shaft of Goliath's spear that hung between his shoulder blades on a rope weighed seventeen pounds (v. 7). To get an idea of how heavy this is, imagine throwing a bowling ball with a wooden shaft attached to it. Goliath's challenge was this: "Choose a man for yourselves, and let him come down to me. If he is able to fight with me and kill me, then we will be your servants. But if I prevail against him and kill him, then you shall be our servants and serve us" (vv. 8–9). This lays down the middleman challenge. "And the Philistine said, 'I defy the ranks of Israel this day. Give me a man, that we may fight together'" (v. 10).

"When Saul and all Israel heard these words of the Philistine, they were dismayed and greatly afraid" (v. 11). Saul and the army of Israel did not see God. All they saw was the Philistine line in front of them and a giant looming over them. They had forgotten the God who was over them. The great tragedy in this event is that not a single person remembered God. Not a single soldier went out to fight Goliath. The text says that this miserable state went on for forty days (v. 16). Forty days passed in which God was simply forgotten.

The Foundation of Honor

How did David honor God in this grand conflict? We see in this story four ways that David honors God in Israel's battle against the Philistines and Goliath. David's honoring of God begins with something that may be unexpected by us moderns, and that is *obedience*. This step is so simple that it is easy to overlook. But David had learned obedience, both to his father and to God. "Jesse said to David his son, 'Take for your brothers an ephah of this parched grain, and these ten loaves, and carry them quickly to the camp to your brothers. Also take these ten cheeses to the commander of their thousand. See if your brothers are well, and bring some token from them'" (vv. 17–18). Jesse gave David plenty of commands— he was to take grain and ten loaves to his brothers. He was also told to take cheeses to his brothers' commander.

David learned from Jesse something that is important for all of us to grasp: obedience to parents. There is a direct link in Scripture between obedience to parents and obedience to God. Jesse most likely taught David from an early age to honor his father and his mother. Through this obedience, David also learned obedience to God. It may sound elementary, but this is the foundation of everything that it means to honor God. Obedience to God's commands expresses that we believe that God is worthy of honor. We show that someone is "heavy" in our life by listening to and obeying that person's commands.

David was eager to obey: "David rose early in the morning" (v. 20). He "left the sheep with a keeper and took the provisions and went, as Jesse had commanded him" (v. 20). David obeyed his father, and in so doing, he obeyed God. When we obey, we put ourselves in the right place to honor God. No one with a track record of honoring the Lord has continually walked in disobedience. Of course, we all sin and disobey, but our response should be to repent, confess our sins, and then walk in a manner worthy of the Lord. It really is as simple as asking the question, "What does God say in His Word, and am I walking in obedience to His commands?" This is the basic building block of what it means to honor God.

Seeing the Unseen God

Second, David honors God by *seeing the unseen God*, unlike the rest of Israel's army. He sees God above the circumstances, above the Philistines, and above the giant. The contrast between David and the rest of the army could not be more striking. The text tells us that "all the men of Israel, when they saw the man, fled from him and were much afraid" (v. 24). They emphasized what they could see: "Have you seen this man who has come up? Surely he has come up to defy Israel" (v. 25). David replies, in essence, "But have you seen God Almighty, Lord of heaven and earth?" David sees all reality with a God-centered lens.

Note David's boldness in his response: "David said to the men who stood by him, 'What shall be done for the man who kills this Philistine and takes away the reproach from Israel?'" (v. 26). Reproach is the opposite of honor. David understands that much more is at stake than the outcome of the battle. God's very honor has been called into question, and shame has been heaped on Yahweh and His army by this pagan giant. This infuriates David because he is acutely aware of the spiritual attack taking place: "For who is this uncircumcised Philistine, that he should defy the armies of the living God?" (v. 26).

What is amazing about David's response is that he is the first Israelite to mention the name of God in the entire story. For David, the sovereign God is seen. God's covenant is remembered. The attributes of God press upon him. This leads David to be concerned about what really matters. He is not just concerned about winning the battle. He is concerned about the honor of God's name. He is angered by the shame that has been poured out on God's name for forty days. He sees everything through the eyes of faith (Heb. 11:1). How is David able to do this?

David tells us his spiritual secret in Psalm 16:8: "I have set the LORD always before me; because he is at my right hand, I shall not be shaken." David intentionally set the Lord always before him. As covenant children of God, we always have God with us: "I am with you always, to the end of the age" (Matt. 28:20). As believers in Christ, we must call to mind that the Lord is with us. David constantly endeavored to remember this truth so that he could face the world without fear. How did David "set the LORD always before [him]"?

In Psalm 19, David declares that both nature and the Word of God declare God's attributes. We can infer that David disciplined his mind to use what he saw in God's creation and what he read in Scripture as prompts to always think about God. He asserts in Psalm 19:1, "The heavens declare the glory of God, and the sky above proclaims his handiwork." In Psalm 19:7, he notes, "The law of the LORD is perfect, reviving the soul; the testimony of the LORD is sure, making wise the simple." David continually read two books: *nature* and *the Scriptures*. In so doing, he practiced this discipline constantly.

As Christians, we also strive to live this way—with a continual vision of God both through nature and through the Scriptures. Everything should point back to Him. We should see God in what He has made, and we should constantly be pursuing God through the Scriptures that He has written. The entirety of the Christian life could be summed up in David's words: "I have set the LORD always before me; because he is at my right hand, I shall not be shaken." This requires that we be disciplined. The Christian life is not "let go and let God," but "I have set the LORD always before me." It takes diligence to open the Word of God and see God. But when we do, we have put on the armor of God to face the challenges of life: opposition from Satan, suffering, and persecution.

Since David lived *coram Deo*—before the face of God—he was able to declare: "The LORD is my light and my salvation; whom shall I fear? The LORD is the stronghold of my life; of whom shall I be afraid?" (Ps. 27:1). We need not fear anything in this world when we are on the side of God. This was David's secret. This was what set him apart from Saul, his brothers, and the rest of the army. He steadfastly kept his spiritual eyes fixed on God.

Persevering through Opposition

Third, David also possessed the courage needed to *persevere through opposition*. When we stand for God's honor, we will be opposed. Our battle is not against flesh and blood but "against the spiritual forces of evil in the heavenly places" (Eph. 6:12). As Christians, we are engaged in a spiritual battle, and those who take a stand for the honor of God will be opposed by the world, the flesh, and the devil—and sometimes even by people close to us who we thought were our friends. It takes courage and fortitude to keep moving forward, and this strength comes from the Lord (v. 13). It is His grace that fuels our fight (2 Cor. 12:9), but it is a fight nonetheless (2 Tim. 4:7). If we are not prepared to persevere through opposition, we will not be effective in living for God's honor.

David encounters opposition almost immediately. The text records: "Eliab his eldest brother heard when he spoke to the men. And Eliab's anger was kindled against David" (1 Sam. 17:28). Eliab is angry because David has shown him up. Eliab should be standing for the honor of God, but he has sat on the bench for forty days. He says to David: "Why have you come down? And with whom have you left those few sheep in the wilderness? I know your presumption and the evil of your heart, for you have come down to see the battle" (v. 28).

Nothing that Eliab says here is true. David is there because Jesse has told him to go and bring provisions. But Eliab essentially says: "I know the presumption of your heart. I know why you're here, that you are evil." Eliab, however, is the one who is presuming. He is presuming to know David's motives. Eliab is the one who has not stood for the honor of God for over forty days, and he is the one with jealous intentions in his heart.

Notice the fortitude with which David responds. "And David said, 'What have I done now? Was it not but a word?'" (v. 29). David did not crumble because he had received criticism. He doesn't say, "Oh, we need to really reconsider what we're doing here in standing for God's honor." Rather, the text says, "And he turned away from him toward another, and spoke in the same way" (v. 30). David did not allow these false accusations to dissuade him. David knew where he stood with God and that he would need to push through the opposition. The need is great in our day that we not back down at the first sign of trouble or criticism. Rather, we need courageous, Spirit-filled Christians who are ultimately consumed with nothing else but pleasing God. The Apostle Paul carried the same mindset, saying, "If I were still trying to please man, I would not be a servant of Christ" (Gal. 1:10). This quality of boldness in the face of opposition is desperately needed today by Christ's saints. It cannot be contrived. It cannot be manipulated. It comes only from spending time with God.

The Stream of God's Honor

Thus far, we have seen that to honor God, we must be obedient, we must see God above the circumstances of our lives, and we must persevere through opposition. But that is not all that David does. Fourth, and most important of all, David puts himself in "the stream of God's honor." What is meant by this phrase? At any given time, numerous spiritual battles are taking place for the honor of God's name. We can be certain that in those battles, God is going to honor His own name, for history will end with the vindication of God's honor. We might not immediately see that vindication, but it will happen. Of course, God allows suffering and setbacks in the present age, but we know how this age ends: "At the name of Jesus every knee should bow, in heaven and on earth and under the earth, and every tongue confess that Jesus Christ is Lord, to the glory of God the Father" (Phil. 2:10–11).

God ends history with the coronation of His honor. Since we know the end of God's grand story, it makes sense to put ourselves in the middle of the stream in which God is moving to honor His own name. Often this means placing ourselves at the point of friction, because the world is pushing in the opposite direction. When we do this, we will be at the intersection of where the Lord can use us to advance His kingdom for His honor. Jesus said, "I will build my church, and the gates of hell shall not prevail against it" (Matt. 16:18). The kingdom advances, Christ's name is praised, and not even hell itself can stop it. What a glorious kingdom to be a part of.

It is critical to remember that God is not currently shaking His head in heaven because there has been a cultural shift in our day. Rather, God is moving history according to His divine timetable, and at the end of that timetable is the honor of God. This is why David does not run from the fight but runs to the fight. He steps out into the valley, sure of the fact that God will honor His own name. David declares to Saul, "Your servant has struck down both lions and bears, and this uncircumcised Philistine shall be like one of them" (1 Sam. 17:36).

Notice David's confidence. He knows that Goliath has "defied the armies of the living God" (v. 36). He sees that this is a fight that God has a vested interest in. David says, "The LORD who delivered me from the paw of the lion and from the paw of the bear will deliver me from the hand of this Philistine" (v. 37). He knows that this battle belongs to the Lord. After David shuns Saul's armor, he takes "his staff in his hand and [chooses] five smooth stones from the brook and put[s] them in his shepherd's pouch" and approaches Goliath (v. 40).

When David finally approaches Goliath, "the Philistine moved forward and came near to David, with his shield-bearer in front of him. And when the Philistine looked and saw David, he disdained him, for he was but a youth, ruddy and handsome in appearance. And the Philistine said to David, 'Am I a dog, that you come to me with sticks?' And the Philistine cursed David by his gods" (vv. 41–43). Notice what Goliath says next and David's rejoinder:

> The Philistine said to David, "Come to me, and I will give your flesh to the birds of the air and to the beasts of the field." Then David said to the Philistine, "You come to me with a sword and with a spear and with a javelin, but I come to you in the name of the LORD of hosts, the God of the armies of Israel, whom you have defied. This day the LORD will deliver you into my hand, and I will strike you down and cut off your head. And I will give the dead bodies of the host of the Philistines this day to the birds of the air and to the wild beasts of the earth, that all the earth may know that there is a God in Israel." (vv. 44–46)

David perceives the battle for what it is, and his confidence is not in himself but in the assurance that God will vindicate His own name. He knows that the battle belongs to God, and he knows where the stream of God's honor is moving. "When the Philistine arose and came and drew near to meet David, David ran quickly toward the battle line to meet the Philistine" (v. 48).

David's tactic is speed. He runs quickly, and then "David put his hand in his bag and took out a stone and slung it and struck the Philistine on his forehead. The stone sank into his forehead, and he fell on his face to the ground. So David prevailed over the Philistine with a sling and with a stone, and struck the Philistine and killed him" (vv. 49–50).

It is remarkable that there is no sword in the hand of David. He then runs and stands over the Philistine and takes Goliath's sword, "and drew it out of its sheath and killed him and cut off his head with it" (v. 51). "When the Philistines saw that their champion [their middleman] was dead, they fled. And the men of Israel and Judah rose with a shout and pursued" them (vv. 51–52). Then "David took the head of the Philistine and brought it to Jerusalem, but he put his armor in his tent" (v. 54).

In dramatic fashion, God vindicated His name. He used a young man so that all the honor would ultimately be His. David was wise enough to see the battle for what it was. He moved to honor God. And in the rest of David's life, we also see the rule of honor displayed. David honored the Lord, and then the Lord honored David. This demonstrates the path that we must all travel in honoring God.

Would David always follow these four steps and honor God? Were there times when he was not in obedience to the Lord and in the stream of God's honor? David sinned against God by committing adultery with Bathsheba and then covering up the sin by having her husband, Uriah, killed in battle. No, David did not always follow these steps, and neither do we. Ultimately, as we will see, the rule of honor leads to the Lord Jesus Christ. He is the only One who completely keeps it and fulfills it.

2

God Honors God

The reality of the God-centeredness of God transforms our understanding of Christianity and even life itself. In chapter 1, we looked at the rule of honor in 1 Samuel 2:30: "Therefore the LORD, the God of Israel, declares: 'I promised that your house and the house of your father should go in and out before me forever,' but now the LORD declares: 'Far be it from me! *Those who honor me I will honor, and those who despise me shall be lightly esteemed*'" (emphasis added).

In articulating this rule of honor, we sometimes hear the accusation that this makes God an "egomaniac" and that He is "self-consumed." Why does God demand that we honor Him? After all, if a human acted this way, we would say that the person had delusions of grandeur. But what we see over and over again in Scripture is that God demands that His name be honored. What is the difference between God and man in this respect?

God Demands Honor

It can be startling to realize that God demands honor. Jesus tells the woman at the well, "The hour is coming, and is now here, when the true worshipers will worship the Father in spirit and truth, for the Father is seeking such people to worship him" (John 4:23). The Father is seeking people to worship Him. That Greek word for "seeking" is *zeteō*, which means "to go after." The Father is "going after" people to worship Him. That is a profound statement. It means that the ultimate goal of our salvation is the worship of God. God is seeking worshipers. In other words, God is seeking God-honorers.

The psalmist declares that "the LORD takes pleasure in those who fear him, in those who hope in his steadfast love" (Ps. 147:11). Have you ever thought about the fact that God takes pleasure in certain things?[1] We think about what pleases us all the time. But what does God take pleasure in? The psalmist points out that God takes pleasure in those who fear His name. This verse is simply a restatement of the first commandment, "You shall have no other gods before me" (Ex. 20:3). God commands us to worship Him and Him alone. He says, "To Me belongs all your worship." Clearly, this is at the very heart of the character of God. God demands that we worship and honor Him. Isaiah 42:8 declares, "I am the LORD; that is my name; my glory I give to no other."

Jonathan Edwards and the Question of God's Demand for Worship

Scripture is clear that God seeks worshipers and that He demands worship. But *why* does God demand that we worship Him? Pastor and theologian Jonathan Edwards helpfully answered this question. Edwards (1703–58) was one of the leading preachers in the First Great Awakening. He tackled this question head-on in his work *A Dissertation concerning the End for Which God Created the World.* The first thing that Edwards established is that God is not a needy, petulant God who needs our worship to complete Him:

> The notion of God's creating the world in order to receive anything properly from the creature is not only contrary to the nature of God, but inconsistent with the notion of creation; which implies a being's receiving its existence, and all that belongs to its being, out of nothing. . . . Now if the creature receives its all from God entirely and perfectly, how is it possible that it should have anything to add to God, to make him in any respect more than he was before, and so the Creator become dependent on the creature?[2]

First, Edwards said that God does not need us to be happy. God is independently happy in Himself. He has never been in dependence on His creation, and He did not need to create the world to add something to Himself. God is always completely satisfied in and of Himself.

Second, Edwards asserted that God always values what is intrinsically most valuable. As a divine and just Judge, God values what is truly valuable and despises what lacks value. Edwards noted, "Whatever is good and valuable in itself is worthy that God should value for itself and on its own account, or which is the same thing, value it with an ultimate value or respect."[3] In other words, God as a perfect Judge values what is most valuable.

Third, Edwards argued that what is most intrinsically valuable must be the end for which the world was created. If God is motivated to pursue what is most valuable, surely this must have been His motivation for creating the world even before the foundation of the world.[4] Having put that together, Edwards pursued his argument in answering the question of why God demands worship and honor:

> That if God himself be in any respect properly capable of being his own end in the creation of the world, then it is reasonable to suppose that he had respect to *himself* as his last and highest end in this work; because he is worthy in himself to be so, being infinitely the greatest and best of beings. All things else, with regard to worthiness, importance and excellence, are perfectly as nothing in comparison of him. And there if God esteems, values, and has respect to things according to their nature and proportions, he must necessarily have the greatest respect to himself. It would be against the perfection of his nature, his wisdom, holiness, and perfect rectitude, whereby he is disposed to do everything that is fit to be done, to suppose otherwise.[5]

That paragraph might be one of the most God-centered paragraphs ever written outside Scripture. Essentially, Edwards says that the highest end of God is God. God esteems Himself most valuable because He *is* most valuable. God esteems Himself most excellent because He *is* most excellent. God esteems Himself most worthy of worship because He *is* most worthy of worship. Edwards goes on to write:

> For God is infinitely and most worthy of regard. The worthiness of others is as nothing to his: so that to him belongs all possible respect. To him belongs the whole of the respect that

any moral agent, either God or any intelligent being, is capable of. To him belongs all the heart.[6]

To God belongs "all the heart." All our worship, all our lives, and all our honor. Edwards is saying that God demands that we worship Him because He alone is worthy. No one else can remotely compare to God. Everything and everyone else is a creature (Rom. 1:25). Everything else is but a drop in the bucket (Isa. 40:15). Nothing else compares to Him.

Edwards observes, "And as the Creator is infinite, and has all possible existence, perfection and excellence, so he must have all possible regard."[7] Since God is ultimate and the most perfect Being, it is fitting that God create beings who might see and rejoice in His perfections. For if it is worthy for God to delight in Himself, then it is worthy and excellent for His creatures to delight in Him also.

This is the great key to joy. The key to happiness is delighting in God. It is rejoicing in what is truly ultimate. As John Piper urges, "Never forget that God is most glorified in you when you are most satisfied in Him."[8] All this is a reiteration of what Paul declares in Romans 11:36: "For from him and through him and to him are all things. To him be glory forever. Amen." God demands that we honor Him because everything is "from him," and therefore everything must point back "to him."

The Perfection of God's Name

One of the ways that God demonstrates His own worthiness is through the revelation of the meaning of His *name*. God explained the meaning of His name to Moses at the burning bush in Exodus 3. At that point, Moses had fled from Egypt and served as a shepherd in the wilderness of Midian for forty years. He was now eighty years old. The text tells us, "Moses was keeping the flock of his father-in-law, Jethro, the priest of Midian, and he led his flock to the west side of the wilderness and came to Horeb, the mountain of God" (Ex. 3:1). Moses called Mount Horeb "the mountain of God" because this was the mountain to which God would lead Moses and the children of Israel and where He would give them the law.

God appeared as a fire in the midst of a bush that did not burn up. As Moses approached the bush, God called out, "Moses, Moses!" And Moses said, "Here I am" (v. 4). God warned Moses, "Do not come near; take your sandals off your feet, for the place on which you are standing is holy ground" (v. 5). By "holy," God means that He is "separate" or "distinct." It speaks to His Godness. The seraphim in heaven call out to one another, "Holy, holy, holy is the LORD of hosts; the whole earth is full of his glory!" (Isa. 6:3).

God is holy because He is God. God is distinct from His creation. He is set apart from us. We are created in His image, but God is "other" in both His perfections and His purity. Like our heavenly Father, we too are called to be holy (1 Peter 1:16). We are called as Christians to be set apart from the world and set apart from the sins of the flesh (cf. Rom. 8:5; 1 John 2:15). We are to be set apart unto God (Eph. 4:1). We are to become like Him (1 Cor. 11:1).

The ground that Moses was standing on was sacred not because the ground itself was special but because God was there.[9] Moses must approach God differently than he would someone else—not flippantly, but with reverence and awe. Moses responded by hiding his face from God (Ex. 3:6). He sensed his own unworthiness and inadequacy. God then told Moses that He had seen the "affliction" (v. 7) of the children of Israel and that He would now vindicate them by remembering His covenant promises to the patriarchs and defeating the Israelites' enemies.

God then revealed His objective to Moses: "Come, I will send you to Pharaoh that you may bring my people, the children of Israel, out of Egypt" (v. 10). Then "Moses said to God, 'Who am I that I should go to Pharaoh and bring the children of Israel out of Egypt?'" (v. 11). God replied, "But I will be with you, and this shall be the sign for you, that I have sent you: when you have brought the people out of Egypt, you shall serve God on this mountain" (v. 12). In other words, one of the ways that God would demonstrate His sovereign providence was by bringing Moses and the children of Israel to that very mountain!

After hearing this news, Moses had a concern: "Then Moses said to God, 'If I come to the people of Israel and say to them, "The God of your fathers has sent me to you," and they ask me, "What is his name?" what shall I say to them?'" (v. 13). Later in the book of Exodus, Moses records that the patriarchs—Abraham, Isaac, and Jacob—had not known the divine name of God (6:3). In this moment when Moses was asked to be God's spokesman, he desired to know the true name of the God who was sending him.

God acquiesced to Moses' request and responded: "I AM WHO I AM. . . . Say this to the people of Israel: 'I AM has sent me to you'" (3:14). God repeated twice a form of the simple Hebrew verb *hayah*, which is the present-tense verb that means "to be" or "I am": *ehyeh asher ehyeh*, "I am that I am." This was God's explanation of His name. Later, the Jews would shorten it to four letters, called the *tetragrammaton*. It is *YHWH* (we often render it as "Yahweh"). This name is so revered by Jews that when they read the Scriptures, they do not pronounce it but instead say *Adonai*, which means "Lord."

God's Aseity

When God declares that His name is "I am," He is stating a mind-blowing truth: "I am self-existent." The theological word for this concept is *aseity*. When I was a child, I would ask my mom, "When did God begin?" She would simply reply, "God has always been." God has always existed, no matter how far back in time we go. In fact, He existed before time was even created. This is what *aseity* means. God is independent, self-existent, and pure Being. While it is impossible for our minds to comprehend this, we must affirm in faith that this is who God is.

God declares, "Remember the former things of old; for I am God, and there is no other; I am God, and there is none like me" (Isa. 46:9). The Puritan Stephen Charnock explained:

> We must come at last to an infinite, eternal, independent Being, that was the first cause of this structure and fabric wherein we and all creatures dwell. The Scripture proclaims this aloud, "I am the Lord and there is none else: I form the light, and I create darkness."[10]

In understanding God's independence, we must come to grips with the reality of our dependence. We exist because of our parents, our grandparents, and numerous providential events that brought them together that go far back into history. We are dependent on the earth being a certain distance from the sun. We are dependent on our atmosphere having oxygen. We are dependent on having fresh water to drink. We are dependent on millions of things, but God is independent. We are here simply because God created us and sustains us. The angels before the throne proclaim, "Worthy are you, our Lord and God, to receive glory and honor and power, for you created all things, and by your will they existed and were created" (Rev. 4:11).

God's Eternality

Another doctrine that flows out of this understanding of God's name is His *eternality*. The Lord Jesus says, "I am the Alpha and the Omega, the beginning and the ending, saith the Lord, which is, and which was, and which is to come, the Almighty" (Rev. 1:8, KJV). Paul describes God, saying: "For his invisible attributes, namely, his *eternal* power and divine nature, have been clearly perceived, ever since the creation of the world, in the things that have been made. So they are without excuse" (Rom. 1:20). In Ephesians 3:11, Paul mentions God's "*eternal* purpose."

Eternality does not just mean that God has existed for all time. It means that God is pretemporal. God is outside time. God is over time. God is not governed by time. Again, this stretches our minds beyond what we can comprehend. We can only think linearly from within time, but even time does not constrain God.

God's Immutability

God's name also refers to the fact that He is unchangeable or, in theological terms, *immutable*. Because God is the essence of existence and is pure Being, He is not in a state of becoming. He is unchangeable in His wisdom, power, holiness, justice, goodness, and truth, and all His other attributes. James teaches, "Every good gift and every perfect gift is from above, coming down from the Father of lights, with whom there is no variation or shadow due to change" (James 1:17). There is not a hint of "variation" in God. There is not even a "shadow" that changes His character or outlook. James tells us that our hope in God's perfect will and in His gifts flows out of this unchangeable, perfect character. If God were changing, there would be no hope that He could actually keep His promises. Praise be to God that this is not the case!

All these divine truths of God's aseity, eternality, and immutability are encapsulated by God's divine name "I am." Therefore, the name of God is to be honored and revered, as is clear in the third commandment (Ex. 20:7). Why is God's name so significant that there needed to be an entire commandment against blasphemy? It is significant because the name of God encompasses all that He is. To spurn the name of God is to spurn God Himself.

Awe for the Name

Later in the book of Exodus, God would demonstrate the heaviness of His name when He brought Moses and the children of Israel back to the very same mountain where God had revealed the divine name to Moses. While Israel was in the wilderness, Moses began to meet with God in a separate tent outside the camp. After Israel's sin with the golden calf, Moses essentially separated himself from the camp (Ex. 33:7). This tent was not the tabernacle but a special tent that Moses used to meet with God, far from the rest of the Israelites.

We read, "Whenever Moses went out to the tent, all the people would rise up, and each would stand at his tent door, and watch Moses until he had gone into the tent. When Moses entered the tent, the pillar of cloud would descend and stand at the entrance of the tent, and the LORD would speak with Moses" (vv. 8–9). The cloud was the visual representation of the presence of God. Then we read something astounding. God would meet with Moses "face to face, as a man speaks to his friend" (v. 11). This is anthropomorphic language that speaks to the intimacy with which God communed with Moses.

In the tent, Moses sought the presence of God and asked Him to continue to accompany the Israelites in the wilderness despite their great sin. Moses told God: "If your presence will not go with me, do not bring us up from here. For how shall it be known that I have found favor in your sight, I and your people? Is it not in your going with us, so that we are distinct, I and your people, from every other people on the face of the earth?" (vv. 15–16).

The Lord responds, "This very thing that you have spoken I will do, for you have found favor in my sight, and I know you by name" (v. 17). All of us would be content with such a commendation from God—to be told that we have divine favor. But Moses pressed further. He wanted an even greater revelation of God's presence. Moses prayed to God, "Please show me your glory" (v. 18). Moses boldly asked to see the essence of God's character because he desired more of the presence of God. God's response to Moses is intriguing: "I will make all my goodness pass before you and will proclaim before you my name 'The LORD' [Yahweh]. And I will be gracious to whom I will be gracious, and will show mercy on whom I will show mercy" (v. 19).

God's Sovereignty

We must not gloss over these words. Here, God is asserting something else implied in His name that we have not yet discussed: His absolute *sovereignty*. Part of this sovereignty is the prerogative to show mercy to whomever He pleases. God will set His goodness on whomever He desires to set it on. He is not bound by anyone. God's favor to Moses does not obligate Him to show favor to anyone else. Often in today's world, our conception of God is that He must show favor to everyone equally without exception. But God says exactly the opposite: He will have mercy on whomever He has mercy.

The Apostle Paul quotes this very statement in Romans 9 in his defense of the doctrine of sovereign election: "I will have mercy on whom I have mercy, and I will have compassion on whom I have compassion" (Rom. 9:15). Paul's argument is that sovereign election to salvation is unconditionally based in the free will of God. Our fleshly response to this assertion is to say, "That's unfair!" Paul anticipates this pushback and simply says:

> But who are you, O man, to answer back to God? Will what is molded say to its molder, "Why have you made me like this?" Has the potter no right over the clay, to make out of the same lump one vessel for honorable use and another for dishonorable use? What if God, desiring to show his wrath and to make known his power, has endured with much patience vessels of wrath prepared for destruction, in order to make known the riches of his glory for vessels of mercy, which he has prepared beforehand for glory—even us whom he has called, not from the Jews only but also from the Gentiles? (Rom. 9:20–24)

Paul's argument is that since God is the sovereign Creator, He possesses the sovereign prerogative to save whomever He chooses. This is for the "glory" of God's name—that salvation is entirely of God and therefore of grace. God asserts this sovereignty to Moses and declares that this too is bound up in His name. When we proclaim God's name, Yahweh, we are also proclaiming His sovereignty.

The Proclamation of the Name

Moses' request to see God's glory took place in the Tent of Meeting. God then instructed Moses to come up onto the mountain, where He placed Moses "in a cleft of the rock." God covered Moses with His hand as He passed by him. Moses saw only the backside of God's presence, not God's face (Ex. 33:22–23). It is hard to understand what this means, since God does not have a body. But what we can say is that God would not show the entirety of His refulgent glory to Moses. Moses was shielded in the cleft of a rock from the Lord's face. When the Lord passed by Moses, He proclaimed His divine name:

> "The LORD, the LORD, a God merciful and gracious, slow to anger, and abounding in steadfast love and faithfulness, keeping steadfast love for thousands, forgiving iniquity and transgression and sin, but who will by no means clear the guilty, visiting the iniquity of the fathers on the children and the children's children, to the third and the fourth generation." (34:6–7)

When Moses heard the divine name, he immediately bowed his head to the ground and worshiped God (v. 8). Moses did so because the divine name is representative of God Himself. Worship is the only proper response to the revelation of who God is. We are to revere God's name because it is the proclamation of His very character. It represents the essence of who He is.

God's Holy Love

In declaring His name, God emphasizes His "steadfast love" and His grace. Both these qualities are also qualities that we possess. We love. We show grace to others. But because God is holy, as we have seen, His love infinitely transcends our love. His love propels Him to mercy. His love leads to our forgiveness. His love prompts Him to send His Son to die as a sin substitute for His people (Rom. 5:8). In fact, John says that we love God and neighbor as we should only "because he first loved us" (1 John 4:19). I emphasize this because people often think that if we emphasize God's holiness, we will then lose the warmth of God's love. In reality, the very opposite is true. God's love is infinite because of His transcendent holiness. It is His transcendence that makes His love infinite. This is the very reason that John says, "God is love" (1 John 4:7).

The Danger of Blasphemy

This clarifies the reason for the third commandment. God's name is to be revered because it encapsulates His holy character. In a scene from *Indiana Jones and the Last Crusade*, Indiana Jones and his father, Henry Jones Sr., have escaped from a German castle where they were held hostage. They are driving in a motorcycle with a sidecar, and they suddenly stop at a crossroads. Henry tells Indiana to make the turn to Berlin so that they can retrieve the grail diary. In the course of the ensuing conversation, Indiana takes

Jesus' name in vain. In immediate response, Henry slaps him. He exclaims, "That's for blasphemy!" The response from Indiana is stunned silence. Henry was right in his response. God's name itself is holy. It represents the essence of God.

While working out at a gym near my house, I heard some young men yelling out God's name in vain every time they dropped their weights on the ground after a set. After this had gone on for a while, I walked over to them and asked them to stop taking God's name in vain—explaining that God's name is to be revered, not used as a curse word. I warned them that by doing this, they were opposing God Himself. They too looked at me in stunned silence. It was probably the first time that they had ever been warned about using God's name in vain. People today use God's name flippantly because they think so flippantly about God. But the more one reveres and loves God's character, the more one will respect His name.

Suffering for the Name

God is so serious about the honor of His name that He even appoints that Christians suffer on behalf of His name. This is because suffering for Christ is one of the greatest tangible expressions of His weightiness. After Paul was converted, Jesus told a man named Ananias to go and lay hands on Paul "so that he might regain his sight" (Acts 9:12). Ananias, knowing Paul's exploits in persecuting the early church, was naturally afraid to approach Paul. "But the Lord said to him, 'Go, for he is a chosen instrument of mine to carry my name before the Gentiles and kings and the children of Israel. For I will show him how much he must suffer for the sake of my name'" (vv. 15–16).

Christ had appointed that Paul would carry His name to the gentiles and that he would suffer much for it. But in the suffering, Paul would demonstrate the greatness of Christ. Later in Paul's ministry, he said that "the Holy Spirit testifies to me in every city that imprisonment and afflictions await me" (20:23). Clearly, God's design for the Apostle to the gentiles was suffering "for the sake of [God's] name" (9:16). Paul goes so far as to say regarding afflictions, "For you yourselves know that we are destined for this" (1 Thess. 3:3).

God demands that He be honored because He is the only One truly worthy of honor. He is the only perfect, timeless, unchangeable, sovereign Being in the universe. Everything that exists flows from and is supported by His Being. Therefore, as Jonathan Edwards made clear, it is only natural that we should be made to worship such a Being, and that our joy should be found in doing so. Honoring God in this dark world will be difficult and will often involve suffering and persecution. But we can be confident because we know that such suffering will bring honor to God's name. Moreover, the rule of honor applies to those who suffer on behalf of Christ. Jesus said:

> "Blessed are those who are persecuted for righteousness' sake, for theirs is the kingdom of heaven.
>
> "Blessed are you when others revile you and persecute you and utter all kinds of evil against you falsely on my account. Rejoice and be glad, for your reward is great in heaven, for so they persecuted the prophets who were before you." (Matt. 5:10–12)

Christ promises to bless and reward those who suffer on account of His name. Rather than being upset, we are to "rejoice and be glad" because such is the extent of our reward.

The Apostles must have taken Jesus at His word, because Luke records that when they were beaten at the hands of the Sanhedrin, they were "rejoicing that they were counted worthy to suffer dishonor for the name" (Acts 5:41). Future honor and suffering go hand in hand. If we are going to honor God, we will eventually suffer for the sake of Christ's name. It could be losing friends because they have departed from sound doctrine. It could be imprisonment because we refuse to compromise on the Bible's sexual ethic. It could be losing property and rights for the cause of Christ. When these things happen, we must remember to rejoice that Christ has counted us worthy to suffer for the sake of His name.

The central theme in all this is that God is worthy. He is worthy of our suffering for and reverencing His name. He is worthy of all honor, glory, and praise. He is worthy because He is the most magnificent Being that exists. As the Apostle Paul succinctly stated, everything is from Him; therefore, everything is to Him (Rom. 11:36).

PART TWO

3

Hiding in Shame

J ohn Calvin opened his famous *Institutes of the Christian Religion* with this statement: "Nearly all the wisdom we possess, that is to say true and sound wisdom consists of two parts, the knowledge of God and ourselves."[1] Calvin was saying that it is only when we understand God truly that we begin to understand ourselves. If we reject the knowledge of God, then we lose aspects of the doctrine of the *imago Dei*, which refers to mankind's being created in the image of God. Rejecting the knowledge of God is like an astronaut's cutting off his tether rope to the space shuttle on his spacewalk. He will only end up free-floating into the abyss of the deep cosmos.

Many people in today's world have divorced themselves from an almighty God and are trying to navigate life without acknowledging their Creator. Cultural decline occurs when people reject God, as is evident in our society's rapidly changing sexual ethics. To understand ourselves rightly, we must do so in the light of God. This is what Paul told the Athenians on Mars Hill: "In him [God] we live and move and have our being" (Acts 17:28). That is the orientation we need—in Him we live and move and have our being. Our modern culture is trying to find that fixed point apart from God and debating what that fixed point can be. But there is no fixed point outside God and His Word.

D. Martyn Lloyd-Jones used to say that "modern man thinks at the same time more highly of themselves than we should and more lowly of ourselves than we should."[2] On one hand, man views himself as inherently morally good at his core. If any deficiency exists, it is the fault of the education system or the home that a person was raised in. Therefore, the solutions to man's problems are therapy and education. In that sense, the modern outlook on mankind is more optimistic than what the Bible says.

But on the other hand, man also views himself as a mere animal evolved from monkeys in a long chain of evolution. There is no afterlife. There is no spiritual reality. We are merely the product of primordial goo. This perspective is too low a view of man. It destroys man's value and *telos* (ultimate end) in the world. According to this view, man is no different from the animals. Lloyd-Jones saw Psalm 8 as the corrective to this faulty outlook.

What Is Man?

David ponders, "When I look at your heavens, the work of your fingers, the moon and the stars, which you have set in place, what is man that you are mindful of him, and the son of man that you care for him?" (Ps. 8:3–4). In other words, David is saying, "When I think about the cosmos and look up at the evening sky, the planets, and the thousands and thousands of stars, how can God even consider man in his insignificance?" The word *mindful* means "inclined to acknowledge or think about." How can God think about a tiny, insignificant creature on this little ball of dust in the cosmos? Moreover, how can God "care" for such a man? David provides the answer in the next verse: God is the One who created us, and our value lies in the fact that God is our Designer:

> Yet you have made him a little lower than the heavenly beings
> > and crowned him with glory and honor.
> You have given him dominion over the works of your hands;
> > you have put all things under his feet,
> all sheep and oxen,
> > and also the beasts of the field,
> the birds of the heavens, and the fish of the sea,
> > whatever passes along the paths of the seas. (Ps. 8:5–8)

Since God is our Creator, humans have value not because we are intrinsically valuable in and of ourselves, but because God is the One who created us. Not only did God create us, but He also created us with dignity distinct from the other creatures. We are "crowned . . . with glory and honor." The crown is an image of royalty that God gives as a royal stamp on us. This language reflects the dominion mandate of Genesis 1:28 and God's command for man and woman to rule the earth. God gives us this crown, this honor, so that we might rule the earth under Him.

In the ancient world, a king would set up a statue of himself in the region that he ruled. That statue would remind all the citizens to submit to and honor his rule. In a similar way, human beings are God's representatives of His rule. God created man and woman as image bearers so that we might take dominion and rule over the entire earth. In Genesis 1:26, God says, "Let us make man in our image." We are to have "dominion" over the entire earth as God's representatives. This is why man is a moral, spiritual, and relational creature.

We are told in Genesis 1 that both man and woman are equal image bearers (v. 27). The gender binary, therefore, is not a social construct invented by modern man. Rather, God created us "male and female." The picture here is that Adam is created as a king and Eve as a helper suitable for him. Eve was to help Adam take dominion of the earth. How? By being fruitful and multiplying (v. 28).

David reiterates these creational truths in Psalm 8 as the reason why God cares so much for man. In response to these great truths, David declares, "O LORD, our Lord, how majestic is your name in all the earth!" (Ps. 8:9). David makes a glorious connection in this last verse: Our honor as men and women made in the image of God directly correlates to the honor of God's name. That single truth explains much of the sin and dysfunction in the world. Our honor is dependent on God's honor because our honor is dependent on His name.

One of the implications of this truth is that if we shame God, we are also bringing shame on ourselves. When we shame God through our sin, we incur shame ourselves. David prays, "O LORD, let me not be put to shame, for I call upon you; let the wicked be put to shame; let them go silently to Sheol" (Ps. 31:17). When we rebel against God, we cut ourselves off from the only honor that we have, and we will incur shame. Lutheran theologian Harold Senkbeil describes shame this way:

> Guilt has to do with behavior, while shame is a matter of identity. Guilt is tied to the sinful things I've done; shame is the

continuous experience of utter remorse over who I am. A person who experiences shame has an abiding sense of failure and self-disgust. We can see how this works in our children. When you correct your child, he is crestfallen because he knows he's done wrong. But he also knows he's disappointed you and therefore has an intense sense of unworthiness. He's ashamed. For his guilt your child needs forgiveness because he knows he has wronged you. For his shame he needs cleansing from his deep sense of defilement and degradation. Maybe he wouldn't be able to put it into words, but inwardly he feels dirty and contaminated in your eyes, and just as he would need a good bath if he fell in a mud puddle, he craves restoration in your sight. So besides forgiving him, when you wrap him up in your arms you reaffirm and embrace him as your beloved son.[3]

Essentially, Senkbeil's argument is that guilt is the result of sin, while shame is the living experience of that guilt. This is why when we commit a sin and it is exposed, shame rushes over us. Shame is the experience we live with after we sin (and in some cases, the experience we live with after someone has sinned against us).

An incident in my childhood illustrates this concept. A friend and I were collecting a bunch of acorns. We climbed the trees in my front yard and started throwing the acorns at the cars going by on the road below. We thought it was great fun until one car came to a screeching halt. A woman opened her door, stepped out into the middle of the road, marched up to my house, knocked on the front door, and told my mom that we had bombarded her car with acorns. As a result, my mom spoke to me those dreaded words, "You wait until your father gets home!" Immediately, a deep feeling of shame rushed over me. I was embarrassed about what I had done and nervous about the punishment that was sure to follow.

We all know what that feeling is. Every sinner—which is every one of us—has experienced it. The *Lexham Bible Dictionary* defines *shame* in this way: "Feelings associated with (but not limited to) failure, public exposure, disgrace, embarrassment, social rejection, ridicule, and dishonor."[4]

One of the signs of moral decline in our culture is that people are now being shamed for doing what God calls morally good. If people stand up for the truth of God's Word, they are often shamed as ignoble opponents of love and human rights. They are called *bigots*. Some even try to expel such people from society. This is all part of Satan's scheme. He wants to silence righteous believers and lead the lost further into real shame. Satan employs simple tactics, and he uses them with great efficiency. He's used one particular tactic since the garden of Eden. First, Satan subverts the Word of God. He then maligns the character of God. If Satan can get us to believe his lies about God's Word and character, he will inevitably lead us into sin and shame.

Satan's Shaming Schemes

Let's look more closely at Satan's schemes with the first man and woman. The first thing that Satan says to Eve is, "Did God actually say, 'You shall not eat of any tree in the garden'?" (Gen. 3:1). God had never said that Adam and Eve couldn't eat of any tree in the garden. Rather, He said that they could not eat of one specific tree—the Tree of Knowledge of Good and Evil. Here, Satan conducts a direct assault on the Word of God, twisting and maligning it, and his strategy has endured throughout human history. Satan wants to get us away from the Word of God, to hide the Word of God, to blaspheme the Word of God, to twist the Word of God, to misquote the Word of God, and to neglect the Word of God.

In the nineteenth century, German biblical scholarship was captured by a movement called *higher criticism*, which studied the Bible with the presupposition that it is simply the words of men and not the words of God. The stories were understood to be myths rather than historical fact. The fish that swallowed Jonah, the serpent that spoke in the garden, the Red Sea that parted as a land bridge for the children of Israel—all were said to be myths. Following the eighteenth-century arguments of David Hume against miracles, higher critics assumed that miracles could not happen.

This cut the heart out of Christianity. Jesus became a historical figure but was not God. There was no room for a literal resurrection from the dead in this scheme. Satan used these brilliant scholars to twist the Bible and subsequently to lead many astray. These same assaults are still happening today. A woman in my church approached me with a letter written by another minister in town in support of homosexual marriage. His argument was that the Scriptures are "not meant to be taken literally." Do we hear the hiss of the serpent in that statement?

But Satan does not stop with an attack on the Word of God. He then launches the second prong of his attack, going directly after the character of God. Satan says to Eve, "You will not surely die" (Gen. 3:4). Here, Satan is essentially calling God a liar. God had already said, "The day that you eat of it you shall surely die" (2:17). But Satan makes it sound as though God has fooled Eve, pulling the wool over her eyes. The reason for this, according to Satan, is that God does not want Eve to know the truth (3:5). Satan claims that once Adam and Eve ate of the tree, their eyes would be opened and they would be wise like God—"knowing good and evil" (v. 5).

Satan blasphemed the character of God. He shamed and brought reproach on the name of God. He marched into God's garden and called God a liar to God's image bearers. That is why when Eve took the fruit it was such a serious violation. It was, as R.C. Sproul frequently said, "cosmic treason against a holy God." It was a direct rebellion against her Creator. It was a public shaming of the name of God.

Four Faulty Responses to Shame

After eating of the fruit, Eve gave some of it to her husband. As a result of this sin, they were immediately overwhelmed by shame. Humans typically try to deal with shame in four ways. The first way is to cover it up. We try to cover our shame because we do not want it to be exposed to the world. Almost immediately, Adam and Eve made loincloths out of fig leaves (v. 7). Shame was the natural and only response that humans could feel after shaming their God. Adam and Eve tried to hide it, and we too want to hide our shame. We understand it for what it is, but we do not want it to be known. As Jesus explained, "For everyone who does wicked things hates the light and does not come to the light, lest his works should be exposed" (John 3:20).

Second, we try to deal with our shame by fleeing from God's presence. When Adam and Eve heard the sound of the Lord in the garden, "the man and his wife hid themselves from the presence of the LORD God among the trees of the garden" (Gen. 3:8). Shame sends people as far as they can go away from God. That's why we have agnostics and atheists, whom the Bible simply calls fools. As David observes in Psalm 14:1, "The fool says in his heart, 'There is no God.'" Atheism in all its forms is always a moral issue. If we have done something wrong and experience that shame, our fallen souls want to avoid God—even His very existence. We avoid darkening the door of a church. We do not want to hear the Word of God because the Word of God reflects His character. We don't want to be around godly people because their lives remind us of ultimate realities. We want to do everything we can to avoid confrontation with a holy God.

Perhaps some of us have experienced the hurt that comes when a friend or family member cuts off a relationship with us because we are Christians. We wonder what happened, and then we find out that the person is living a life of sin. He or she has pulled back because of the shame. The person does not want to be around us because our very presence is a reminder of God. This phenomenon explains why there is such a backlash and even hatred toward truth. All truth flows directly from the character of God. Even if we speak the truth in love, the truth causes great discomfort to someone who is living in shame. Apart from the Holy Spirit's doing an inside work of the heart, that person does not want to hear the truth.

But the reality is, no matter how hard we try, we cannot flee from the presence of God. We cannot hide ourselves from God's presence. Every square inch of His creation testifies to His existence. There is nowhere we can go from His presence. The psalmist cries out: "Where shall I go from your Spirit? Or where shall I flee from your presence? If I ascend to heaven, you are there! If I make my bed in Sheol, you are there!" (Ps. 139:7–8). We can never escape God. There was nowhere in the garden that Adam and Eve could go to escape the presence of God. Running from God is always an illusion.

The third way that we try to deal with shame is by pursuing a life of lostness because shame leads us to think more lightly of ourselves. We begin to view ourselves as morally profligate. God can use this lostness to lead the lost to Himself, but often, like the Prodigal Son, the lost will not experience this until they hit rock bottom. The experience of shame often drives the sinner to even more shameful deeds. This is part of the rule of honor. God gives us over to our shame—to things that ought not to be done. A long cycle of shameful acts follows, whereby the sinner keeps throwing himself into his sin. Adam and Eve did not try to go to God with their sin; instead, they hid from Him "among the trees of the garden" (Gen. 3:8). But graciously, in Adam and Eve's case, God intervenes: "The LORD God called to the man and said to him, 'Where are you?'" (v. 9). Obviously, God knows exactly where they are, but He is pressing them with the reality of their lostness.

Fourth, we try to deal with our shame by blame-shifting. Confronted by God, Adam says, "The woman whom you gave to be with me, she gave me fruit of the tree, and I ate." When God spoke to Eve, she said, "The serpent deceived me, and I ate" (vv. 12–13). They both blame others for what they have done. Adam blames the woman, and he also blames God for giving her to him. The woman blames the serpent. This is often our last resort when dealing with shame and being confronted about our actions. "It was someone else's fault," we tell ourselves.

The Only Way to Deal with Shame

The problem with the strategies above is that none of them actually work. None of them actually deal with our shame. The only way for us to rightly deal with this feeling of shame is to go back to God. We have no recourse to cover our own shame. Everything that man tries to do to deal with shame is simply fig leaves, hiding in trees, pursuing lostness, and blame-shifting. What we need is for God to come and deliver us. As the Apostle Paul puts it in Colossians 1:13–14, "He has delivered us from the domain of darkness and transferred us to the kingdom of his beloved Son, in whom we have redemption, the forgiveness of sins." This is the only hope for dealing with our shame—God's deliverance.

Understanding our need for God's deliverance undergirds God-centered Christianity. Man-centered Christianity tries to give practical steps that people can take to deal with their own problems. God-centered Christianity points sinners to God, who is the only One adequately equipped to redeem us. God-centered Christianity understands the severity of sin and thus the necessary supernatural remedy of God's intervention in our lives. The law of God is given to us so that our mouths may be stopped before God (Rom. 3:19). Our sin is revealed so that we may realize that we are sinners in need of a Savior. God must redeem us. God must cover our shame.

After Adam and Eve sin, God does exactly that: "The LORD God made for Adam and for his wife garments of skins and clothed them" (Gen. 3:21). God sacrifices animals on behalf of Adam and Eve, clothing them with garments of skin. God intervenes to take away their shame. The only way for Adam and Eve to no longer be naked is for God to clothe them. But this clothing is costly—requiring the lives of animals. This all points forward to what the Lord Jesus would do. The greater Son of Adam and Eve would crush the serpent's head (v. 15).

The Shame of the Tree

When Adam and Eve hid in the garden, they hid among the trees. Where did Jesus go to deal with our shame? The tree of Calvary. This is what Paul emphasizes in Galatians 3:13: "Christ redeemed us from the curse of the law by becoming a curse for us—for it is written, 'Cursed is everyone who is hanged on a tree.'" It is hard to imagine the shame that the Lord Jesus Christ endured while He was on the cross. The One who deserves all the honor in the universe was shamed by the very humans He created. God made Him who knew no sin to be sin on our behalf (2 Cor. 5:21). Jesus suffered the public embarrassment and ignominy that we deserve for our sins.

Most scholars and historians of the crucifixion believe that Jesus was crucified naked on the cross. The Gospels tell us that He was crucified right outside the city gate, next to a road. People walked by on that road, scoffing at Him (Matt. 27:39; Luke 22:65). It was a public spectacle. A public embarrassment. He endured it in order to take our shame on Himself so that He might redeem us from the curse of the law by becoming a curse for us.

Adam and Eve failed to honor God in the garden and subsequently hid behind trees. Jesus honored God for thirty-three years and then resolutely set His face toward the tree in Jerusalem to incur our shame. The writer of Hebrews says that we are to look "to Jesus, the founder and perfecter of our faith, who for the joy that was set before him endured the cross, despising the shame, and is seated at the right hand of the throne of God" (Heb. 12:2).

He despised the shame. He persevered through it. He endured it so that He might perfect our faith and lead us shamelessly into the throne room of God. Paul went as far as to declare, "For the Scripture says, 'Everyone who believes in him will not be put to shame'" (Rom. 10:11).

It's important to note that our sense of shame could not be taken away if our guilt still remained. The primary thing that our Lord accomplished at the cross was to pay the penalty for sin that we deserved. Sometimes theologians call this understanding of the atonement *penal substitution*. This doctrine states that Christ died in our place, taking the punishment that we deserve for our sin (Rom. 3:24–25; 2 Cor. 5:21). Without the removal of guilt through Christ's blood, all the shame and ignominy of our sin would still be on us. In other words, the removal of shame is a *result* of penal substitution, not a separate theory of the atonement that stands on its own. My friend Aubrey Sequeira, who ministers in Abu Dhabi, has noted the tendency for missionaries to not emphasize penal substitution in honor/shame cultures, focusing instead only on the honor/shame itself.[5] This is a huge mistake, because as we noted earlier, shame is tied to guilt. You cannot take away shame without first taking away guilt.

We can all think back to shameful things that we have done and the experience of shame that accompanied them. As believers, we must remember that Christ has borne our guilt and thus taken away our shame. This is the freedom of the gospel. Whenever God-centered Christianity is rediscovered, there is always a renewed understanding of the depths of our own guilt and shame. We see our sin for what it is—a public shaming of God that deserves nothing but shame in return.

Without a proper understanding of sin, we cannot understand Christ's substitutionary work. And if we lose Christ's substitutionary work, we lose the gospel itself. We must face the reality of our guilt and shame head-on, because only then will we see the wonderful reality of the cross. For the gospel to be seen as glorious, our shame must be seen as inglorious. Only in that light will we appreciate our Shame-Bearer, the God-man, the Lord Jesus Christ.

4

The Weightiest Steps

I ain Murray once said: "The Bible no more knows a separate class of heroes than it does of saints. Because of Jesus Christ, every Christian is extraordinary and attains to glory. Yet grace so shines in some as in the portraits of Hebrews 11, that it lightens the path of many."[1] In other words, what really helps us in the Christian life is being able to look at someone else and follow in his or her footsteps. Maybe this person is three years ahead of us, or five years, or ten years. At some point in our lives, most of us have looked at the life of a godly believer and thought to ourselves, "I want to be like that person!"

No one envisions the future without looking to examples of those who have gone before. That is how God wired the learning process to work. For example, when I was a freshman in the Corps of Cadets at Texas A&M, I looked up to certain student leaders who were in the classes ahead of me. I found their presence and leadership on campus remarkable. Names such as Tim Bailey, Paul Terrell, Ryan Bishop, Keaton Askew, Patrick Hebert, and Will Whitehurst come to mind. They served as models for the person

I wanted to become. To achieve what they had achieved, I needed to imitate their character and actions. So it is in all of life.

In terms of ministry, I have had so many influences and models that it is hard to mention them all. My father-in-law, Carl Broggi, taught me almost everything I know about practical ministry. When I was a high school student, the Lord used John MacArthur's preaching on the radio to call me into pastoral ministry. I am an expository preacher today because of his ministry. In my early years in the Marine Corps, I was introduced to the ministry of R.C. Sproul. I listened to his CDs for hours, driving around in my truck. I owe much of my theological thinking to him.

But perhaps no one has been more important in my approach to ministry than Dr. Martyn Lloyd-Jones. Affectionately called "the Doctor" because he was a physician, he ministered at Westminster Chapel in London from 1939 to 1968. Though he died in 1981, three years before I was born, I have consumed his books and listened to hundreds of his sermons. While doing some summer studies in England, I had the privilege of visiting Westminster Chapel. One of the deacons showed me the vestry just behind the sanctuary, where Lloyd-Jones would pray before services and meet with parishioners afterward. To my surprise, in the vestry closet was the very Genevan gown that Lloyd-Jones had worn while preaching. It was still there in the chapel more than fifty years later.

To be able to hold that gown was a weighty moment for me. Though I don't believe I will ever live up to Lloyd-Jones' life, I aspire to be faithful to the Word of God as he was faithful to the Word of God. I aspire to stand against theological drift as he stood against drift. And most importantly, I aspire to finish my course of ministry well, as he finished his.

The Weightiest Life

Yet all human examples we could cite are ultimately insignificant when compared to the life of our Lord Jesus Christ. Our Lord walked with the weightiest of steps. Paul states this in Philippians 2:9–11: "Therefore God has highly exalted him and bestowed on him the name that is above every name, so that at the name of Jesus every knee should bow, in heaven and on earth and under the earth, and every tongue confess that Jesus Christ is Lord, to the glory of God the Father." That is a remarkable statement about someone who is truly a man and is also Lord and God, and worthy of worship.

This point was brought home to me in a fresh way when I was a college student. Hanging on the outside wall of the auditorium I used to study in was a mural of the whole timeline of human history. I would always position myself directly in front of this timeline because I loved to look at the different events of history chronologically. I was captivated by the fact that the Lord Jesus was the most prominent feature of it. It clearly showed that Christ and His cross were the dividing line of history. The marker between "Before Christ" and "Anno Domini" (In the year of our Lord) was most prominent. Every time I looked at it, it reminded me in a tangible way that Christ is Lord of history and that all history must be understood in light of Him.

God-centered Christianity understands the weightiness of Christ's life. Jesus Himself said, "If anyone would come after me, let him deny himself and take up his cross daily and follow me" (Luke 9:23). As much as we follow other people as models, those models are only as good as their conformity to Jesus Christ. Paul urges in 1 Corinthians 11:1, "Be imitators of me, as I am of Christ."

He can say that because he himself is imitating Christ. Similarly, we can sincerely tell others to follow us only if Christ dominates our own lives. He is the ultimate model.

The question often asked, especially by unbelievers, is: "Why does Jesus deserve to be followed? Why are His steps the weightiest?" The answer goes all the way back to the rule of honor articulated in 1 Samuel 2:30: "Those who honor me I will honor." What did Jesus do in His life to deserve to be honored with the highest name? He honored the Father perfectly. He honored Him in such a way as to deserve the highest honor. He honored God in a way that no human being before or since has ever done.

In John 8, the Pharisees accuse Jesus of being born from "sexual immorality" (John 8:41). They also accuse Him of being possessed by a demon (v. 48). Jesus' answer is telling: "I do not have a demon, but I honor my Father, and you dishonor me" (v. 49). That one phrase, "I honor my Father," is such a remarkable statement because He is the only One who can truly say such a thing. We all have fallen short of God's righteous standard, whereas Jesus displayed the weightiness of God in everything He did. Every second of time, every ounce of His strength, every moment of His day, from His birth to His ascension into heaven, He honored the Father. No one has ever been more reverently God-centered than Jesus. No one has ever glorified God more than Jesus. Jesus perfectly honored the Father. Even the greats of the Old Testament, such as Moses, David, and Elijah, fell far short of the perfect standard set by the Lord Jesus.

In chapter 1, we noted four ways that David honored God. Matthew takes great pains in his genealogy to show the connection between David and Jesus (Matt. 1:6). Jesus is the son of

David, and Jesus honors God as His father David did, albeit in a much grander way. But like David, Jesus was first obedient to His parents and ultimately to God. Like David, Jesus saw God above all earthly realities. He persevered through immense opposition. And like David, Jesus put Himself in the stream of God's honor. How is Christ the greater David? Let's turn to that now.

The Obedient Son

Of the four Gospel accounts, Luke has the only record of Jesus as a child. All that we know of Jesus' boyhood is found in Luke 2: "And the child grew and became strong, filled with wisdom. And the favor of God was upon him" (v. 40). The word "strong" that Luke uses is the same word that John uses in his first epistle: "I write to you, young men, because you are strong, and the word of God abides in you, and you have overcome the evil one" (1 John 2:14). This indicates that the type of strength Luke refers to in Luke 2:40 is spiritual strength. It is a strength to overcome temptation, a strength in the Word of God, a strength of communion with God. All these "strengths" Jesus possessed to an exceptional degree even as a boy.

Luke 2 also records that during this time, Jesus went with His family to celebrate the Passover in Jerusalem. When they left to go back to Nazareth, and after an entire day on the road, they realized that Jesus was nowhere to be found (v. 44). His parents went back to Jerusalem, and after searching for Him for three days, they finally found Him in the temple, "sitting among the teachers, listening to them and asking them questions" (v. 46). Jesus then reminded Joseph and Mary that He was to be found in His "Father's house" (v. 49). Such was His devotion to honor and commune with God. Then Luke records something remarkable. He says that after this, "he went down with them and came to Nazareth and was submissive to them" (v. 51). Jesus was obedient to Mary and Joseph.

Even at the earliest point recorded about His childhood, Jesus demonstrated obedience to both God and His parents by obeying the fifth commandment. Obedience would be the pattern of His whole life.

My Food Is to Do the Will of the Father

It is through this lens of obedience to the Father that Jesus understood His mission. He went so far as to say, "My food is to do the will of him who sent me and to accomplish his work" (John 4:34). Obeying the will of God was Jesus' food. It was the daily bread He ate. It's what got Him up in the morning. Jesus was driven by a resolute desire to be obedient to the Father. In John 5:30: He declares, "I seek not my own will but the will of him who sent me." In John 6:38, He says, "For I have come down from heaven, not to do my own will but the will of him who sent me." In John 8:28, Jesus asserts to the Jewish leaders, "When you have lifted up the Son of Man, then you will know that I am he, and that I do nothing on my own authority, but speak just as the Father taught me." In John 12:49, He says, "For I have not spoken on my own authority, but the Father who sent me has himself given me a commandment—what to say and what to speak." Then in John 14:10, He asks: "Do you not believe that I am in the Father and the Father is in me? The words that I say to you I do not speak on my own authority, but the Father who dwells in me does his works."

Clearly, one of the central themes of Jesus' ministry in the gospel of John is that all His words and deeds were according to the will of the Father. It was a perfect life of obedience, so much so that Paul describes Jesus' life this way in Philippians 2:8: "And being found in human form, he humbled himself by becoming obedient to the point of death, even death on a cross." Jesus' obedience extended to the cross. His death was the final and ultimate demonstration of His obedience. The writer of Hebrews notes, "Although he was a son, he learned obedience through what he suffered" (Heb. 5:8). Jesus demonstrated the depth of His obedience at Golgotha. While He could have called down an army of angels at any minute during His suffering, He endured it willingly, fulfilling the will of the Father. When commenting about the law in the Sermon on the Mount, Jesus explained it to His disciples this way: "Do not think that I have come to abolish the Law or the Prophets; I have not come to abolish them but to fulfill them" (Matt. 5:17). Jesus is emphasizing that He came to obey the entire law perfectly, without one false note. There was not one blemish. Not one stray word. Not one naughty look. It was perfect obedience all the way through. Jesus fulfilled the law and honored God through righteous obedience.

A Vision for God

In addition to His perfect obedience to the Father's will, Jesus also maintained a transcendent vision of God. He saw the Father above every situation, and He viewed everything in light of the character of God. Jesus maintained a laser focus on the reality of the kingdom of God. He was and is truly the most God-honoring and God-centered individual to have ever lived. He was so dedicated to this vision of God that He allowed nothing to push Him off course or to distract Him.

This is modeled in how Jesus approached and communed with God in prayer. Isn't it striking that the Son of God spent so much time in prayer? We might assume that as the Son of God, the second person of the Godhead did not need to pray. But Jesus frequently communed with the Father in prayer throughout His life. Mark records at the beginning of his gospel, "And rising very early in the morning, while it was still dark, he departed and went out to a desolate place, and there he prayed" (Mark 1:35). After Jesus had fed the five thousand and "after he had taken leave of them, he went up on the mountain to pray" (6:46). Luke informs us that before Jesus chose the twelve disciples, "He went out to the mountain to pray, and all night he continued in prayer to God. And when day came, he called his disciples and chose from them twelve, whom he named apostles" (Luke 6:12). Before the transfiguration, "about eight days after these sayings he took with him Peter and John and James and went up on the mountain to pray" (Luke 9:28). And in the garden of Gethsemane, Jesus withdrew from His disciples and knelt down, and there He prayed (22:39–46). Jesus lived His entire life out of the overflow of this communion with God.

This enabled Jesus to keep His focus on God through everything He encountered. Numerical success never went to His head. In fact, He often prevented and repudiated the type of numerical success we crave. When Jesus' mother asked Him to make wine at the wedding in Cana, Jesus said to her: "Woman, what does this have to do with me? My hour has not yet come" (John 2:4). In Jesus' ministry, "hour" refers to the divine timetable on which

He operated. His rebuke essentially meant that even though she was His mother, He could not be coerced to do works outside of God's divine plan. It was not impressing people that He was concerned about, but doing God's will.

After Simon Peter's confession at Caesarea Philippi that Jesus is the Christ, Matthew records, "From that time Jesus began to show his disciples that he must go to Jerusalem and suffer many things from the elders and chief priests and scribes, and be killed, and on the third day be raised" (Matt. 16:21). Jesus focused on His objective to offer Himself as a sacrifice for sinners through His death. At this point, He sat His disciples down and told them explicitly what would happen to Him. His complete focus was on honoring God through His atonement. Now that they grasped His lordship, it was time for the disciples to understand His mission.

Jesus taught us to live with the same type of vision for God. The Lord's Prayer begins: "Our Father in heaven, hallowed be your name" (Matt. 6:9). The prayer opens with the honor of God, reminding us that there is a God in heaven whose name is to be revered. Jesus is teaching us to lift up our eyes from our own circumstances and to fix our eyes on God, who is in heaven. He's above our reality. He's transcendent. And our desire should be to see His name honored. In this way, the beginning of the Lord's Prayer shows us how Jesus lived. This was His vision. This was how He saw the world—with God over everything.

Satan's Temptations

One of the great questions that we must all answer is, "How do I respond when I face opposition?" The proverb observes, "If you faint in the day of adversity, your strength is small" (Prov. 24:10).

When the going gets tough, how do we respond? When we are tempted, how do we respond?

After Jesus is baptized, His ministry begins with a forty-day fast in the wilderness—one day for every year that Israel was in the wilderness. Jesus essentially recapitulates Israel's history. Israel went into the wilderness after being baptized in the Red Sea; Jesus went into the wilderness after being baptized in the Jordan River. Whereas the Israelites failed in the wilderness by grumbling and complaining (Ex. 16), Jesus does not.

Jesus is hungry after forty days, and at this point of physical weakness, Satan comes to Him and tells Him to turn the stones into bread (Matt. 4:3). In response, Jesus quotes Deuteronomy 8:3: "Man shall not live by bread alone, but by every word that comes from the mouth of God" (Matt. 4:4). In other words, "God's Word is true, and My sustenance is to take in His Word and promises."

In the second temptation, Satan tells Jesus to throw Himself down from the Temple Mount. Satan quotes the portion of Psalm 91 that says God will charge His angels concerning Him. Satan quotes Scripture, but if we read all of Psalm 91, the psalmist speaks about how Satan will be overthrown (Ps. 91:13). Satan doesn't quote that verse! Rather, he selectively quotes Psalm 91, encouraging Jesus to willfully put Himself in danger so that God can rescue Him. The event would create a spectacle and a following for Jesus. It is a temptation of religious pride. Jesus quotes Deuteronomy, saying, "Again it is written, 'You shall not put the Lord your God to the test'" (Matt. 4:7).

The third and final temptation Satan delivers is a temptation to have the kingdom without the cross. Satan seeks to persuade Jesus to receive all the kingdoms of the world without walking the road to Calvary. All Jesus must do is to bow down and worship Satan (Matt. 4:9). Satan promises, "All these I will give you, if you will fall down and worship me" (v. 9). Jesus replies to him: "Be gone, Satan! For it is written, 'You shall worship the Lord your God and him only shall you serve'" (v. 10). Jesus shows Himself faithful through every temptation.

Opposition from His Inner Circle

Jesus not only succeeded where Israel failed. He also succeeded where Adam failed. Adam was tempted in the garden and failed, but Jesus succeeded in the wilderness after fasting for forty days. Jesus overcame all of Satan's opposition. At times, Jesus was also opposed by His own family. Mark records that when Jesus' family heard about His ministry and miracles, "they went out to seize him, for they were saying, 'He is out of his mind'" (Mark 3:21). How hard would it be to continue in your work if your own family claimed that you were out of your mind? Such was the opposition that Jesus faced. They came to the house where He was staying and called to Jesus to come out (v. 31). They were staging a family intervention on Jesus' ministry.

Jesus answered them, "Who are my mother and my brothers?" And looking about at those who sat around him, He said, "Here are my mother and my brothers! For whoever does the will of God, he is my brother and sister and mother" (vv. 33–35). Notice how Jesus does not even flinch. He simply responds by saying, "These are My mother and brothers and sisters." Nothing is going to stop Him from carrying out His mission. Not even His family.

Jesus also overcame opposition from His own disciples. Immediately after Peter confesses that Jesus is the Christ at Caesarea

Philippi, as we saw earlier, Jesus tells them that He is going to the cross, and "Peter took him aside and began to rebuke him, saying, 'Far be it from you, Lord! This shall never happen to you'" (Matt. 16:22). The very Apostle whom Jesus had just commended for his declaration of Christ's lordship presumes to grab Him by the collar, take Him aside, and rebuke Him. Essentially, Peter is telling Jesus the same thing that Satan told Jesus earlier during His temptation: that the kingdom was to be inaugurated without the cross. That's why Jesus then admonishes Peter: "Get behind me, Satan! You are a hindrance to me. For you are not setting your mind on the things of God, but on the things of man" (v. 23).

Satan stood in Jesus' way. His family stood in His way. His own disciples stood in His way. And in the Gospels, we find verse after verse of opposition and confrontation with the Pharisees and the Sanhedrin. He was falsely accused and arrested by them. He was beaten, mocked, and scourged. Yet Jesus faithfully persevered through all this spiritual and institutional opposition.

The Stream of God's Honor

Jesus clearly put Himself in the stream of God's honor. He came to this world in love and compassion, but what ultimately drove Him was the honor of God. His compassion to save sinners flowed from this desire. He desired "to seek and to save the lost" (Luke 19:10), but His highest desire was that God's name would be honored.

One great example of this is Jesus' cleansing of the temple at the beginning of His ministry. Jesus found money-changers and sellers of oxen, sheep, and pigeons for sacrifices (John 2:14). This upset Jesus because they were not supposed to be doing that in the Court of the Gentiles. It was not against the Jewish law to convert currency for the temple tax or to sell animals for sacrifices to Jewish pilgrims. The problem was that they brought all those filthy animals and put them in the place where the gentiles were supposed to come and worship.

When Jesus cleared the Court of the Gentiles, He was vindicating the honor of God's house. He was motivated by a desire for God's worship to be revered. The text says: "And making a whip of cords, he drove them all out of the temple, with the sheep and oxen. And he poured out the coins of the money-changers and overturned their tables" (v. 15). Jesus then told the pigeon sellers, "Take these things away; do not make my Father's house a house of trade" (v. 16). He was consumed with the honor of God's name. "His disciples remembered that it was written, 'Zeal for your house will consume me'" (v. 17).

Jesus was consumed by the honor of God. This is at the heart of God-centered Christianity. Notice that no one else rose up with Jesus. He flipped the tables alone. He poured out the coins of the money-changers alone. He chased out the vendors alone. He alone was consumed with the honor of God. In this, we see our Lord's example, calling us forward. Sometimes being in the stream of God's honor means that we will act alone. But what is most important is that God's name be honored above all.

Jesus understood this. It is why He went to the cross to die—for the honor and glory of God. Jesus understood the cross to be the greatest demonstration of God's honor and glory because on the cross, the grace, mercy, love, and justice of God would all be displayed. In John 13:31–32, Jesus declared: "Now is the Son of Man glorified, and God is glorified in him. If God is glorified in him, God will also glorify him in himself, and glorify him at once."

Jesus understood the cross as the apex of both God's glory and His own glory. Yes, He went to the cross to save us. But He also went to the cross to vindicate the name of God and to demonstrate the glory of God (Rom. 3:21–26).

This was the drumbeat of Jesus' life and ministry, every step demonstrating the weightiness of God. He put Himself at the point of friction—in the stream where God's name would be honored. He marched toward Jerusalem, not away from it. He lived a God-centered life as no one before Him ever had and as no one else after Him ever has or ever will. That is why He has the weightiest steps and why "at the name of Jesus every knee [will] bow . . . and every tongue confess that Jesus Christ is Lord, to the glory of God the Father" (Phil. 2:10–11).

5

The Shamed Christ

We have seen that God must honor God and that God demands that we honor Him as well because He alone is worthy of honor. This is our divine purpose for being created. Anselm of Canterbury understood this well. Anselm was a monk who lived in Normandy of France. He later became archbishop of Canterbury in 1093, when he was sixty years old. He died about sixteen years later, in 1109.

Anselm was a brilliant thinker in the realm of apologetics, but perhaps his greatest contribution came through his doctrine of the atonement in his book *Cur Deus homo*, which translated from the Latin is *Why the God-Man?* In the book he answers the question, "Why did God become a man?" Anselm's primary thesis is that each person owes a debt to God because of his or her sin. We have each failed to give God the honor that is due Him, and the Lord Jesus paid the debt that we owed to God through His substitutionary death. According to Anselm:

This is the sole honor, the complete honor, which we owe to

God in which God demands of us. Someone who does not render to God this honor due to him is taking away from God what is his and dishonoring God, And this is what it is to sin. As long as he does not repay, he remains in a state of guilt.[1]

According to Anselm, we owe honor to God. We were created to honor God, have utterly failed in that endeavor, and thus have sinned. Anselm goes on to say, "Everyone who sins is under an obligation to repay to God the honour which he has violently taken from him, and this is the satisfaction which every sinner is obliged to give to God."[2]

As we saw earlier, we must understand sin primarily in a judicial sense—that Jesus died to pay for our guilt before God (Rom. 3:25). Certainly, that is the basis for our understanding of the atonement. What is striking about Anselm's understanding of the atonement is that it is vertical. For modern man, sin is horizontal. For Anselm, sin is primarily vertical and in relation to God. And we must understand sin in a vertical sense before we can understand it in a horizontal sense.

Every single sin is an affront against a holy God, and every single sin is a failure to give God the honor that He is due. Therefore, each and every person is living in God's debt. Anselm says, "There is nothing more intolerable in the universal order than that a creature should take away honor from the Creator and not repay what he takes away."[3] That is a God-centered perspective on reality. There is nothing more intolerable than taking away honor from our Creator.

Moreover, as we have seen, the Scriptures teach that sin brings shame, which is the opposite of honor. As Solomon puts it in Proverbs 14:34, "Righteousness exalts a nation, but sin is a reproach to any people." Sin always brings reproach and shame. It is the red-hot embarrassment we feel when we get caught. It is the ignominy of having our mug shot appear on the front page of the newspaper. It is the humiliation of being caught in the act. It is being treated lightly by our friends, family, and coworkers as a result of something that we did.

David describes this reality in Psalm 44:13: "You have made us the taunt of our neighbors, the derision and scorn of those around us." Neighbors taunt us when they feel that we are worthless—when our honor has been diminished. David goes on to say: "You have made us a byword among the nations, a laughingstock among the peoples. All day long my disgrace is before me, and shame has covered my face" (vv. 14–15). That is what it means to be shamed. We become a disgrace to both God and man. Such is the shame that we have all experienced before God.

Another thing that we learn from Anselm's understanding of the atonement is the doctrine of substitution. Christ honors God in our place. Christ suffers the shame we deserve in our place. This is how the writer of Hebrews understood the atonement: "Let us run with endurance the race that is set before us, looking to Jesus, the founder and perfecter of our faith, who for the joy that was set before him endured the cross, despising the shame, and is seated at the right hand of the throne of God" (Heb. 12:1–2). The word translated "despising" could be translated as "looking down on something that you dread pushing through."

Jesus saw the shame of the cross as something that He had to endure for us and ultimately "for the joy that was set before him." That joy would come from redeeming us and from executing His

Father's will. In short, Jesus endured the shame of the cross for us. According to Anselm, that is *why* the God-man came. It was substitution: Christ's suffering for us, paying for our guilt, and then taking away our shame.

The Shame of Betrayal

After Jesus instituted the Lord's Supper with His disciples in the upper room, they sang a hymn and walked across the Kidron Valley to the garden of Gethsemane (Matt. 26:30). It was a place where Jesus was known to pray, and He and His disciples had likely spent the night there when they were in Jerusalem. Judas knew that he could find Jesus there (John 18:2). While in the garden that evening, Jesus dedicated His time to prayer and communion with God. He took Peter, James, and John a short distance from the other disciples, and He began to pray in agony to God.

Three times He came back to the three disciples and encouraged them to pray, but each time they fell asleep (Matt. 26:37–45). At this point, Jesus said, "Rise, let us be going; see, my betrayer is at hand" (v. 46). Judas came into the garden with a "great crowd" (v. 47). John informs us that accompanying Judas was "a band of soldiers and some officers from the chief priests and the Pharisees" (John 18:3).

The first act of shame that took place in the garden was the betrayal by Judas. To be betrayed is by definition shameful. It means to be handed over by someone in our inner circle that treats us so lightly that he or she double-crosses us. Judas came to be defined by this act of shame. That is why he is called "the betrayer." He committed the shameful act of betrayal against our Lord by giving Him a betraying kiss.

John says that after the kiss, "the band of soldiers and their captain and the officers of the Jews arrested Jesus and bound him" (John 18:12). Jesus thought it was odd that they bound Him as though He were a dangerous criminal: "Have you come out as against a robber, with swords and clubs to capture me? Day after day I sat in the temple teaching, and you did not seize me. But all this has taken place that the Scriptures of the prophets might be fulfilled" (Matt. 26:55–56).

Shortly after this incident, Judas was so overcome with his own guilt and shame that he took the thirty pieces of silver (which he had been paid for betraying Jesus) and tried to give it back to the Pharisees and the high priest, but they would not take the money. So Judas threw it into the temple, and he went to a field and hanged himself. Meanwhile, Jesus was taken from Gethsemane back across the Kidron Valley into the city of Jerusalem. John then tells us something that the other Gospels don't mention. Jesus' captors first took Him to the house of the old high priest, whose name was Annas (John 18:13). Annas, the father-in-law of Caiaphas, was a living legend to the Jews and had been deposed by the Romans. He was really the one pulling the strings on everything. While waiting to meet with Annas, Jesus was shamed by one of His closest disciples, Peter.

Peter denied the Lord once in the courtyard of Annas and twice in the courtyard of Caiaphas (Matt. 26:57–75; John 18:15–18, 25–27). According to New Testament scholar Leon Morris, it is also possible that Annas and Caiaphas shared the same palace and courtyard or that Caiaphas simply could have initially been visiting Annas' palace. So this could have been exactly the same place.[4] Regardless, it is hard to grasp how the very disciple who had seen the Lord Jesus transfigured in all His glory on the Mount of Transfiguration (Luke 9:28–36) could now deny Him. The very disciple who had exclaimed in Matthew 16:16, "You are the Christ, the Son of the living God," the one who had declared in John 6:69 that "we have believed, and have come to know, that you are the Holy One of God," is the same one who now denied even being associated with the Lord Jesus Christ. But such was the weight of the shame that was heaped on our Lord by the Jews that Peter simply succumbed to it all. He denied his Lord rather than being associated with Him.

The Hearing with Annas

Annas questioned Jesus, trying to get Him to condemn Himself with His own words (John 18:19). Jesus answered him: "I have spoken openly to the world. I have always taught in synagogues and in the temple, where all Jews come together. I have said nothing in secret" (v. 20). Jesus was essentially saying: "Look, if you want to know what I teach, just go and ask the people; they have been hearing Me teach in the temple and in the synagogues for My entire ministry. I don't have any secret teaching that I've kept from the world. Everyone has heard what I've said!" He then boldly stated: "Why do you ask me? Ask those who have heard me what I said to them; they know what I said" (v. 21).

After He rebuked Annas, Jesus was slapped by one of the high priest's attendants, who said, "Is that how you answer the high priest?" (John 18:22). Jesus responded, "If what I said is wrong, bear witness about the wrong; but if what I said is right, why do you strike me?" (v. 23). In other words, Jesus was saying: "If what I said is wrong, prove it with witnesses. You have heard Me speak publicly. There are plenty of witnesses! But if I am right, then why the strike?" In all this shaming, Jesus held His ground—responding with honor while being shamed. Peter, later reflecting on this episode in the Lord's life, states in 1 Peter 2:22–24:

> He committed no sin, neither was deceit found in his mouth. When he was reviled, he did not revile in return; when he suffered, he did not threaten, but continued entrusting himself to him who judges justly. He himself bore our sins in his body on the tree, that we might die to sin and live to righteousness. By his wounds you have been healed.

Blasphemy against Christ

After questioning Jesus, Annas sent Him to Caiaphas' palace, where the Sanhedrin was gathered (John 18:24). Mark tells us that everybody was waiting for Jesus at Caiaphas' house at close to 4 or 5 in the morning (Mark 14:53). The Sanhedrin was not supposed to meet on the eve before a Sabbath or a feast day, so this was a phony trial from the beginning, filled with shameful injustices. The Sanhedrin treated Jesus more like a doomed animal than a human. Luke notes that while Jesus was in the courtyard, before the members of the Sanhedrin met, they played a game of human piñata with Him. They blindfolded Him, and then they started turning Him while punching Him and spitting on Him, mocking Him (Luke 22:63). While hitting and spitting on Him, they shouted: "'Prophesy! Who is it that struck you?' And they said many other things against him, blaspheming him" (vv. 64–65). Blasphemy is akin to verbal shame. They treated Jesus with as much disdain as they possibly could. They felt devilishly vindicated when the Lord would not prophesy according to their silly demands.

After Jesus endured the public shaming and beating in the courtyard, He then stood trial before the Sanhedrin. Under Jewish law, two witnesses were required to convict someone of a crime, so they brought forth false witnesses to try to convict Jesus. Since witnesses were not allowed to listen to the testimony of other witnesses, one witness at a time was brought in. They all completely contradicted one another (Mark 14:56). Finally, in desperation, Caiaphas asked Jesus, "Are you the Christ, the Son of the Blessed?"

Jesus said, "I am, and you will see the Son of Man seated at the right hand of Power, and coming with the clouds of heaven" (vv. 61–62). The Jewish leaders knew exactly what Jesus was saying here. The "Son of Man" was the apocalyptic figure from Daniel 7, the Messiah, the Son of God Himself. Upon hearing that, the high priest tore his robe and said to the Sanhedrin, "What further witnesses do we need?" (v. 63)—in other words, "This man has blasphemed; He's called Himself God." At this, they began beating Him and striking Him relentlessly and yelling at Him to "prophesy!"

Only the poured-out blood of Jesus in death would satisfy the leaders' anger. But there was just one problem. The Jews, under Roman rule, were not allowed to inflict capital punishment. They had to obtain a guilty verdict under Roman law for capital punishment to be carried out. This is why they brought Jesus to Pilate in the early-morning hours of Friday (John 18:28). This had been their plan all along—thus the meeting of the Sanhedrin in the middle of the night. When they got to Pontius Pilate, the Roman governor of Judea, he did everything he could not to pass down a guilty verdict on Christ. At least one of the reasons for this was that during the night, Pilate's wife had had a dream, and in that dream, she was warned to have nothing to do with Jesus (Matt. 27:19).

From Blasphemer to Insurrectionist

What is fascinating is the charge that the Jewish leaders brought to Pilate. The charge they had brought before the Sanhedrin was blasphemy, but they brought a completely different charge to Pontius Pilate. They accused Jesus of insurrection because He claimed to be a king. Luke records: "They began to accuse him, saying, 'We found this man misleading our nation and forbidding us to give tribute to Caesar, and saying that he himself is Christ, a king'" (23:2). The Jewish leaders knew that the Messiah was a king because they knew about all those claims from the Old Testament. They knew that Jesus had claimed to be ushering in the kingdom of God. So they switched the charge to something that they thought Rome would punish. Rome did not care about a charge of blaspheming a Jewish God. Hundreds, if not thousands, of gods were worshiped throughout the Roman Empire. What the Romans did care about was what every king and dictator in the history of politics cares about: a threat to their rule.

The Sanhedrin charged Jesus with essentially the same thing. This is how they put their thumb on Pilate and pressured him into passing a guilty verdict. Of course, Pilate tried to avoid the trap by sending Jesus to Herod. But Herod, after mocking Jesus and arraying Him in fine clothes, sent Him right back to Pilate (Luke 23:11). Pilate had to deal with this charge of insurrection, as well as the mounting accusations from the Jews that if he were to release Jesus, he too would be guilty of treason.

Trying to figure a way out, Pilate took Jesus aside and questioned Him about the nature of His kingdom. Jesus made this reply: "My kingdom is not of this world. If my kingdom were of this world, my servants would have been fighting, that I might not be delivered over to the Jews. But my kingdom is not from the world" (John 18:36). Pilate latched on to Jesus' statement that He has a kingdom, asking in verse 37, "So you are a king?" And Jesus answered: "You say that I am a king. For this purpose I was born and for this purpose I have come into the world—to bear witness to the truth. Everyone who is of the truth listens to my voice" (v. 37).

Pilate then uttered this famous question: "'What is truth?' He then went back outside to the Jews and told them, 'I find no guilt in him'" (v. 38). No truer words have ever been spoken. There was not one ounce of guilt in our Lord. But the Jewish leaders and the people held this charge of insurrection over Jesus and pressed Pilate all the more. Pilate, in a desperate attempt to negotiate with the crowd, offered to let Jesus go free by putting forward a notorious criminal named Barabbas.

In a show of envy and hate, the crowd chose Barabbas. Eventually, Pilate put his hands into a wash basin and declared, "I am innocent of this man's blood; see to it yourselves" (Matt. 27:24). In one of those great statements of theological irony, the crowd responded, "His blood be on us and on our children!" (v. 25). Then Pilate gave Jesus over to be crucified.

A Crown of Ignominy

When someone received a sentence of crucifixion, a flogging almost always followed the sentence. They went hand in hand.

It was part of what made the execution method so gruesome. So according to custom, Pilate gave Jesus over to be scourged (Mark 15:15). This would have been brutal in and of itself and could even result in death.

After this horrendous torture, Jesus was shamed by the entire Roman battalion—about six hundred Roman soldiers. Mark records that "they clothed him in a purple cloak"—a garment that was reserved for royalty—"and twisting together a crown of thorns, they put it on him" (v. 17). What happened next is both remarkable and unusual for the treatment of a criminal. When I was in the Marine Corps, there was a custom for when a dignitary, such as a president or a senator, came to visit the base. We performed a military parade with the distinguished individual on a reviewing stand. The entire battalion or regiment would march in front of the reviewing stand, and as each company and platoon reached the reviewing stand, they would turn their eyes to the right and salute the reviewing officer. The gesture of "eyes right" and the salute was a great honor to bestow on someone.

What the Roman battalion essentially did was to place the Lord Jesus in the exact place where the reviewing and inspecting officer would stand. They placed a crown of thorns on His head, and then they conducted a mock military parade. Mark records that they saluted Him and shouted, "Hail, King of the Jews!" (v. 18). Then they bowed before Him while spitting on Him and beating Him with a reed (v. 19). It was perhaps the most shameful act that has ever been committed in history: the Lord of glory being humiliated by an entire Roman battalion in a mock parade—spitting on their Creator. And when they had mocked

Him, they stripped Him of the purple cloak and put His own clothes on Him. "And they led him out to crucify him" (v. 20).

The Shame of the Cross

After being flogged, every person to be crucified would have to carry his own cross. Jesus had noted this fact in Luke 9:23: "If anyone would come after me, he must deny himself and take up his cross daily and follow me." The individual had to pick up that crossbeam, weighing up to 150 pounds, and carry it to the place where he would be crucified. Jesus came out of Pilate's headquarters on what is now called the *Via Dolorosa*, "the way of suffering." He walked, carrying this heavy beam, but in His state of physical exhaustion, He could not make it all the way to the crucifixion site. The authorities then ordered a man named Simon of Cyrene to carry His cross (Matt. 27:32; Mark 15:21; Luke 23:26). Simon carried Jesus' cross outside the city gate to a place called Golgotha.

It was at Golgotha (which means "Place of a Skull") that Jesus was crucified (Matt. 27:33; Mark 15:22; Luke 23:33; John 19:17). Crucifixion was an execution method designed by the Persians, practiced by the Greeks, and perfected by the Romans. It served as the feared method of sustaining Roman domination—shamefully and excruciatingly punishing Rome's political enemies. That was the point. Execution by beheading with the sword would be too quick. The Romans wanted their enemies to be shamed. That was the point of the cross.

The details of a crucifixion are grisly. The Romans would strip their prisoners of all their clothes—they were crucified completely naked in most cases. The Romans took every piece of clothing off the doomed person to heighten his shame, and then they nailed him to the cross. They put nails through his wrists and feet, and the only way for the person to get oxygen was to pull himself up, exerting pressure on those nails. Fire would course through the nerves in the arms and legs when that pressure was exerted, yet the crucified man would have to do just that: pull himself up to breathe, and only then let himself down, to begin suffocating again.

The condemned man would do that again and again until he died of suffocation or exposure. Sometimes this process of slowly dying could take days. It was the most painful and shameful way that a person could ever be killed, bringing meaning to what Paul says in Galatians 3:13: "Christ redeemed us from the curse of the law by becoming a curse for us—for it is written, 'Cursed is everyone who is hanged on a tree.'" The custom in Old Testament Israel, after someone had been stoned to death because he had committed a capital offense, was to place his body on a pole for all to see (Deut. 21:22). The purpose of this exposure was to bring public shame to the individual. Moreover, the hanging body served as a visible symbol to the people of Israel of the judgment of God for grievous sin. Paul makes the symbolism explicit in Galatians 3. Christ became a public curse for us. His hanging body on the cross shows us the wrath of God for our sin. His shame before God and the world is the shame that we should bear because of our guilt. Christ truly became the very picture of the curse for us on the cross.

After Jesus was crucified, the Roman soldiers cast lots for His clothes (Mark 15:24). This had been predicted in Psalm 22 more than a thousand years earlier, when David said that the Messiah would be treated with so much ignominy that people would gamble over His clothes. Moreover, they crucified Him between two thieves, fulfilling what the prophet Isaiah had foretold that He would be "numbered with the transgressors" (Isa. 53:12; see Matt. 27:38; Mark 15:27; Luke 23:32–33). Of course, the real insurrectionist, Barabbas, was supposed to be on the middle cross. They put Jesus on the cross where the real criminal was supposed to be crucified—a vivid picture of substitution. Pilate had a sign placed above Jesus' head with an inscription that read "King of the Jews" in Aramaic, Greek, and Latin (Matt. 27:37; Mark 15:26; John 19:19).

Jesus was crucified on the road going into the city, and many who walked on the road mocked Him for the first three hours on the cross. Mark records that those who passed by on the road "derided him," saying, "You who would destroy the temple and rebuild it in three days, save yourself, and come down from the cross!" (Mark 15:29–30). "So also the chief priests with the scribes mocked him to one another, saying, 'He saved others; he cannot save himself. Let the Christ, the King of Israel, come down now from the cross that we may see and believe'" (vv. 31–32). And if that weren't enough shame, the Scriptures record that even the thieves mocked Him: "the robbers who were crucified with him also reviled him" (Matt. 27:44; see also Mark 15:32). Jesus was publicly shamed by all classes of people—the Romans, the Jewish elites, and even the criminals. The shame was universal in its scope. Of course, Luke recounts that one of those thieves would eventually repent, turn to Christ, and defend Him (Luke 23:40–43).

But another shame is seen at the cross that dwarfs the others. Darkness pervaded the land for three hours, from noon until 3 p.m. (the sixth hour until the ninth hour) (Matt. 27:45; Mark 15:33; Luke 23:44). "At the ninth hour Jesus cried with a loud voice, 'Eloi, Eloi, lema sabachthani?' which means, 'My God, my God, why have you forsaken me?'" (Mark 15:34). In quoting the opening words of Psalm 22, Jesus was describing the theological reality of His own experience. On the cross, He was experiencing the divine punishment for guilt in our place. As Paul explains in 2 Corinthians 5:21, "For our sake he made him to be sin who knew no sin"—not that Jesus became a sinner but that He bore our punishment for our sins on the cross.

A vertical transaction was taking place in this moment. The wrath that we deserved was poured out on Him. Thus, the foulness of our shame draped His soul. The stench of our sin covered His sinless body. The penalty that we deserved He paid. The shame that we deserved He wore. This is why He said, "It is finished," right before He died (John 19:30). He had thoroughly accomplished what would have taken us an eternity in hell to do. When He had paid for our sin, our Lord gave up His life. It was not that He died as a result of a broken heart; rather (and this point must be stressed), He gave up His own life for ours. "He bowed his head and gave up his spirit," John records (v. 30).

We sometimes fail to understand the deep guilt and shame of our own sin. We discount it. We excuse it. We justify it. But Jesus died for it. Every one of our sins is one for which Christ died. In this sense, David was right in Psalm 51:4 when he said, "Against you, you only, have I sinned." Ultimately, sin must be seen as a violation against God that must be paid for by God Himself. That is why it is so treacherous and despicable.

Jesus endured this guilt and shame to purify a bride so that she would be "without spot or wrinkle" (Eph. 5:27). He did this in love (Rom. 5:8). The cross is the greatest demonstration of the love of God (1 John 4:10). It helps us understand why the prophet said that even our righteous deeds are like filthy rags (Isa. 64:6). They are nothing compared to Christ's righteous life and work. There is no possible way in our own righteousness to take away the guilt and the shame that sin has brought on us.

This understanding of the cross is central to recovering God-centered Christianity. The cross demonstrates the value of God's honor. It magnifies the great weightiness of God. It highlights the holiness of God. God is so weighty that God Himself had to redeem us so that we would be saved. We are constantly reminded of the great majesty of God by looking at the cross. Nothing less than the shameful death of His own Son was necessary to vindicate it. If we minimize sin, that means we have a very small vision of God and therefore a very truncated understanding of the cross. It is at the cross that we see God in all His glory.

In reflecting on the shame of the cross, the Apostles didn't end their discussion of Jesus' shame at Golgotha. Paul declares that because Jesus absorbed such great shame, He deserves the highest honor. For this reason, Paul says that his response to Jesus' shame is "my eager expectation and hope that I will not be at all ashamed, but that with full courage now as always Christ will be honored in my body, whether by life or by death" (Phil. 1:20). We honor Him because He took away our shame. This is the great motivation of the Christian life. Our guilt and shame were taken away so that we can live for His honor.

Paul encourages the church at Colossae, "And you, who once were alienated and hostile in mind, doing evil deeds, he has now reconciled in his body of flesh by his death, in order to present you holy and blameless and above reproach before him" (Col. 1:21–22).

This is the ultimate meaning of the cross. Christ takes away the guilt and shame of His people. That's why the Son of God came. He did not come merely to teach us the ethic of the kingdom of God. Nor did He come simply to model a God-centered life, though He certainly did. He came ultimately to take away our guilt through His substitutionary death on the cross. In the words of Anselm, this is the *why* of the God-man.

PART THREE

6

The Honor
of the Christian

The Apostle Paul tells us in Romans 3:12, "All have turned aside; together they have become worthless; no one does good, not even one." He goes on to make a blanket statement in Romans 3:23: "All have sinned and fall short of the glory of God." That's why Jesus Christ came into this world—to keep the rule of honor and fulfill it on our behalf. He honored God perfectly in His completely righteous life, and He went to the cross and suffered the shame and punishment that we deserved. He died in our place for our sins. This, along with the good news of Christ's resurrection, is the central message of Christianity (1 Cor. 15:3–4).

It is through faith in Christ alone that God credits us with all of Christ's work. So when we hear the rule of honor ("Those who honor me I will honor, and those who despise me shall be lightly esteemed"; 1 Sam. 2:30), we must recognize that only the true Christian who has trusted in Christ is on the good side of the rule. It's only through His perfect life, death, and resurrection that we can be honored by God. The moment that we trust in Christ, a transformation occurs. We move from a place of shame to a place of honor. Now God can honor us—not on the basis of our own work, but on the basis of Christ's work. Peter puts it this way: "So the honor is for you who believe" (1 Peter 2:7). This, above everything else, is what makes Christianity unique from every other religion. In all other religions, you stand on your own merit. In Christianity, we stand on the fact that Christ has taken our guilt and shame and given us His earned righteousness and honor.

Bestowed Honor

We all know what it means to be honored. We see Heisman Trophy winners and Grammy and Oscar winners every year. Every field has its distinct honors. When I was a student at Texas A&M, I took several classes in the agricultural department. I soon learned about a famous scientist named Norman Borlaug, who happened to still teach at the university. Borlaug was famous because he had biologically engineered a new wheat strain that had saved billions of lives over the past sixty years.

As a result of this great accomplishment, Borlaug won the Nobel Peace Prize in 1970, and then in 1977 the Presidential Medal of Freedom. In every agronomy class I took, he was revered and his name spoken with a sense of awe. When he was seen walking in the halls or across campus, everyone wanted to meet this great man. He was bestowed with honors upon honors. Now, suppose, hypothetically, that Borlaug had engineered that wheat strain, had been awarded all the great honors, but did not know that they had been given to him. How do you think his life would have been different if he had never heard of the distinctions that he had been given? We assume that his life would have been lived very differently.

Unfortunately, in a spiritual sense, that's how so many Christians live their lives—oblivious to the honors that have already been bestowed on them in Christ. To understand the honor that has been given to us, we must understand some of the basic honors that the New Testament speaks about.

The Honor of Sainthood

The first honor is the honor of *sainthood*. If you have ever visited the Vatican or stepped foot in a Roman Catholic church, you will have noticed that the stained-glass windows often have pictures of various saints on them. In Roman Catholic theology, a saint is someone who achieved super-meritorious works—whose life was so holy that he or she provided extra merit (beyond what was needed to reach heaven) that could then be given to others by the Roman Catholic Church.

In Roman Catholic theology, the greatest saint who lived the most meritorious life is Mary, the mother of Jesus. She is called "the Virgin Mary," but we know from the Gospels that she had many other children with Joseph (see John 7). Mary is considered by Rome to be even greater than the Apostles. In fact, Rome claims that she was preserved from the taint of original sin from the moment of her conception—in a doctrine called the *immaculate conception*—and also that she remained free of personal sin throughout her life. In Roman Catholic theology, both Jesus and Mary are sinless. Her sainthood is so exalted that she is even said to be able to intercede for us in a priestly manner, like Jesus Christ. Of course, only a few people are ever officially recognized as saints by Rome. There might be a St. Benedict or St. Francis every few hundred years, but these are extremely rare individuals whose sainthood the Roman church recognizes.

Contrary to that theology, the New Testament teaches that every single Christian is honored with the title *saint*. Furthermore, this title is given to believers even in light of the fact that we are still sinners. Even Mary was a sinner. The Gospels record one point at which she doubted our Lord's ministry and tried to bring Him home (Matt. 12:46; Mark 3:31). Mary was a sinner who needed salvation and Christ's imputed righteousness, just like everyone else.

The sainthood of the believer is taught by all the Apostles, but one of the places it is most clear is in Paul's first letter to the Corinthians. Paul begins that letter by saying, "To the church of God that is in Corinth, to those sanctified in Christ Jesus, called to be saints together with all those who in every place call upon the name of our Lord Jesus Christ, both their Lord and ours" (1 Cor. 1:2). Notice that this title of "saint" is given in reference to the people's relationship to Christ. The saints are those who have been "sanctified in Christ Jesus."

Clearly underlying this statement is the doctrine of justification by faith—that believers are counted righteous in Christ through faith apart from their own works. Thus, the title "saint" became the Apostle Paul's favorite way to describe the Christian (see Rom. 1:7; 2 Cor. 1:1; Eph. 1:1; 2:19; Phil. 1:1; Col. 1:2, 26; etc.). It is "in Christ" that Christians are sanctified, or cleansed, of all their sin. It is in Christ that we are credited with all of Christ's good works. Therefore, we must make an important distinction here. This sainthood that Paul is talking about is not conditioned on our becoming more holy. It is conditioned only on the fact that the Christian is declared holy through faith by virtue of what Christ has already accomplished.

How do we know this? First, because the Corinthian church had severe issues. A man in this church was living in incest (see 1 Cor. 5:1–2). The church was fraught with immorality of all sorts (v. 11). Clearly, the Corinthians' title of "saints" was not based on their performance. Second, Paul says in 1:30 that "you are in Christ Jesus, who became to us wisdom from God, righteousness and sanctification and redemption." The sanctification that he's speaking about here is explicitly based on the finished work of Christ. He says in verse 2 that we are sanctified in Christ Jesus and "called to be saints together." That word "called" means "appointed." The Apostle says that God has "appointed" us to be saints. The word "saint" means "holy one"—one who is set apart unto God. Remarkably, this is the word that Paul uses to describe every single Christian.

There are two important implications of our sainthood. First, the reality of sainthood has a massive impact on how we treat and care for other Christians. If every single Christian is a saint, that means that we are to "bear one another's burdens, and so fulfill the law of Christ" (Gal. 6:2). We are to treat one another as saints. We are to honor other Christians. We are to go out of our way to help them. We must be careful not to sin against them, disparage them, or slander them, for they are saints.

Second, if we are truly saints, then we are to live as such. If our identity is that of saints, then this should compel us to live as saints in this world. This is similar to Paul's point in Romans 6:3–4, where he says in essence, "Do you not know who you are, that you've been buried with Christ in His death, that you've been raised to walk in newness of life?" Paul states in Titus 2:11–12,

"For the grace of God has appeared, bringing salvation for all people, training us to renounce ungodliness and worldly passions, and to live self-controlled, upright, and godly lives in the present age." The grace of God trains us to live the Christian life because it is who we are now. In Christ, we are saints. That is our identity. To go back to our old way of life would be preposterous. We are saints, so we must live like saints.

The Honor of Being a Friend of God

The second honor bestowed on the Christian is that of being a *friend of God*. In Adam, we are naturally enemies of God, morally hostile to Him. We are born rebels, standing against His reign. No one is born on good terms with God. By nature, we are enemies of God. Paul proclaims in Romans 8:7, "For the mind that is set on the flesh is hostile to God, for it does not submit to God's law; indeed, it cannot." In Colossians 1:21–22, Paul points out, "And you, who once were alienated and hostile in mind, doing evil deeds, he has now reconciled in his body of flesh by his death." In Romans 5:10, Paul goes so far as to call us "enemies" of God.

We must understand that the world that we live in is *not* neutral ground. We've been taught the faulty notion that the public square is neutral and that people are naturally morally good, but nothing could be further from the truth. The Bible teaches that we are either a child of God or a child of the devil—part of the kingdom of Christ or part of the kingdom of darkness (John 8:40–46). There is no middle ground. There is no neutral camp. We are either a friend of God or an enemy of God. We are either at peace with God or at war with God.

We begin our lives as enemies of God, but what happens in conversion and through justifying grace is a glorious change in our status. A great honor is bestowed on us. As Paul puts it in Romans 5:1, "Therefore, since we have been justified by faith, we have peace with God through our Lord Jesus Christ." This peace that Paul speaks about is not subjective. It is not a feeling. Rather, it is an objective reality that we have entered into. Our status has completely changed, from enemy to friend. Abraham was called a "friend of God" (James 2:23). And everyone who, like Abraham, believes the promises of God in Christ is also counted as a friend of God. We who were once hostile enemies are now counted as God's friends.

Many believers do not realize that in Christ, they have this objective peace with God. So many think that when they sin, God is just waiting to strike them down with a thunderbolt from heaven, or even to take their salvation away from them. They worry that God will react to their sin and treat them as His enemy. But if we are in Christ by faith, we are forever under terms of peace with God. We are God's friend, and we will always be His friend.

When we understand this status of being a friend of God, it changes how we think about our relationship with Him. When I was in the Marine Corps, I was stationed in Japan. We often worked with the Japan Self-Defense Forces and heard stories about Japanese soldiers after World War II who never surrendered. They were out on a Pacific island somewhere, and they never got the news that World War II had ended. In fact, they did not hear until years later that terms of peace had been reached.

One Japanese soldier, named Hiroo Onoda, continued to conduct military operations in the Philippine jungle until

1974—twenty-nine years after the war had ended! Once his whereabouts finally became known, his former commanding officer was dispatched to find him, relieve him of his duties, and bring him back to mainland Japan. Of course, peace between America and Japan had already been established for twenty-nine years. Yet Onoda was not aware of this. He did not realize that he was under terms of peace.

A similar tragedy occurs from a spiritual standpoint when we do not realize that we now live under terms of peace purchased by Christ. That's why James urges: "Draw near to God, and he will draw near to you. Cleanse your hands, you sinners, and purify your hearts, you double-minded" (James 4:8). If we have trusted in Jesus, we must stop thinking that we are enemies of God when we are actually His friends. We can confess our sins, repent of them, and draw near to God because we have restored fellowship with Him. We need not stay distant, because though we were once God's enemies, we are now His friends.

This is what Paul expresses in Romans 5:10: "For if while we were enemies we were reconciled to God by the death of his Son, much more, now that we are reconciled, shall we be saved by his life." In other words, the ascended Christ now intercedes for us at the right hand of God the Father so that we can continue to have this reconciliation with God the Father. We are friends of God in Christ, and we will always be friends of God from now unto eternity (see John 15:15). Jesus, at the right hand of the Father, ensures it.

The Honor of Being a Child of God

Third, every Christian has the honor of being a *child of God*. John says in John 1:12, "But to all who did receive him, who believed in his name, he gave the right to become children of God." This honor is given only to those who receive the Lord Jesus Christ in faith, who believe in His name.

Jesus declares in the Sermon on the Mount: "Therefore do not be anxious, saying, 'What shall we eat?' or 'What shall we drink?' or 'What shall we wear?' For the Gentiles seek after all these things, and your heavenly Father knows that you need them all. But seek first the kingdom of God and his righteousness, and all these things will be added to you" (Matt. 6:31–33). He observes a few verses later, "If you then, who are evil, know how to give good gifts to your children, how much more will your Father who is in heaven give good things to those who ask him!" (7:11).

Good parents take care of their children. Jesus' argument is this: If we know how to take good care of our children, how much more will our heavenly Father take care of us! We live under the kind, providential hand of a loving Father, and that outlook gives perspective to our circumstances. When we endure a tough time and wish that our circumstances were different, we can know in those moments that our heavenly Father has us exactly where we are supposed to be. Every moment is ordained by God for our good (Rom. 8:28; Eph. 1:11). That is a remarkable reality in which we live—knowing that God, as our Father, has us exactly where we are supposed to be.

In addition to God's sovereign provision as Father, God has also promised a heavenly inheritance for His children. Paul points out in Galatians 4:7, "So you are no longer a slave, but a son, and if a son, then an heir through God." Most of us have heard stories about people who suddenly find out that they have inherited an unexpected fortune. Spiritually speaking, this is the reality that every single child of God has entered into. Every Christian is an heir. What is our inheritance? Paul tells us, "Blessed be the God and Father of our Lord Jesus Christ, who has blessed us in Christ with every spiritual blessing in the heavenly places" (Eph. 1:3). Every single blessing in the heavenly places is ours if we are children of God. When we understand the eternal blessings that await us in heaven, the things of this world start to fade away pretty quickly.

The bumper sticker that reads "He who dies with the most toys still dies" is true. Paul says in 1 Timothy 6:7, "For we brought nothing into the world, and we cannot take anything out of the world." Jesus made this promise before He ascended into heaven: "If I go and prepare a place for you, I will come again and take you to myself, that where I am you may be also" (John 14:3). Jesus is preparing a place for us. He is preparing spiritual blessings for us. This life is a brief vapor, and death often awaits us around unexpected corners. The things of this world do not compare with the spiritual blessings that we will inherit (2 Cor. 4:17). Therefore, Paul reminds us to "look not to the things that are seen but to the things that are unseen. For the things that are seen are transient, but the things that are unseen are eternal" (v. 18).

The Honor of the Indwelling Holy Spirit

A fourth honor that the Christian receives is *baptism with the Holy Spirit*. Some Christians may not realize that they have been baptized with the Holy Spirit because some segments of modern Christianity teach that the baptism of the Holy Spirit is a "second blessing" that not every Christian receives. But that is not true. Every believer is baptized in the Holy Spirit (1 Cor. 12:13). The teaching of the baptism of the Spirit is often confused because Luke presents the baptism of the Spirit as taking place *after* conversion in the book of Acts. But if we study Acts carefully, we realize that Luke is going to great lengths to show us that all different types of Christians receive this gift. Jesus commanded the disciples to be "witnesses in Jerusalem and in all Judea and Samaria, and to the end of the earth" (Acts 1:8). Not surprisingly, then, Luke shows various ethnic categories of Christians receiving the Holy Spirit.

Acts begins with Jesus about to ascend into heaven. He promises in Acts 1:5, "John baptized with water, but you will be baptized with the Holy Spirit not many days from now." Forty days later, the Apostles and many other Jews are baptized with the Holy Spirit (Acts 2). But the baptism of the Holy Spirit is not isolated only to the Jews. In Acts 8, Philip goes and evangelizes the Samaritans; the Apostles subsequently come and lay hands on the Samaritans, and they too receive the Holy Spirit (Acts 8:17).

God-fearing gentiles also received the Holy Spirit, as we see in Acts 10 when Cornelius and his whole house believe and receive the Holy Spirit: "While Peter was still saying these things, the Holy Spirit fell on all who heard the word" (v. 44). By the end of Acts 10, the Holy Spirit has baptized Jews, Samaritans, and God-fearing gentiles. But it doesn't stop there. Just as Jesus promised, the witness will go to the outermost parts of the earth—to the pagan gentiles. This occurs in Acts 19 when Paul goes to Ephesus. The Ephesian Christians had received only the baptism of John the Baptist but not the baptism of the Spirit, so Paul lays hands on them, and they also receive the Holy Spirit (19:6).

This is why Paul notes in 1 Corinthians 12:13, "For in one Spirit we were all baptized into one body—Jews or Greeks, slaves or free—and all were made to drink of one Spirit." Every single believer, regardless of ethnic origin, is baptized into the Spirit. This is why the book of Acts describes these varied episodes of baptism in the Spirit. It does not teach a "second baptism" as normative, but rather the opposite: every believer is baptized with the Holy Spirit.[1]

As new covenant believers far removed from these events in the book of Acts, we might be tempted to think that there's not much special or surprising about believers' being indwelled by the Holy Spirit. We must recognize that the baptism of the Holy Spirit is a profound honor for the new covenant believer. Under the old covenant, only prophets, priests, and kings were baptized with the Holy Spirit. To be sure, the Holy Spirit regenerated all old covenant saints. But His normative spiritual presence was experienced at the tabernacle, and later in the temple. Individual baptism was experienced only by the special officers and priests of Israel. Even then, there was no guarantee of a perpetual baptism. After David's sin, he was afraid that God would take the Holy Spirit from him: "Take not your Holy Spirit from me," he prayed (Ps. 51:11).

Therefore, under the new covenant, it is a tremendous honor that every believer is given the baptism of the Holy Spirit. This means that the new covenant believer does not require a temple or a tabernacle to meet with God. Rather, His presence is with us wherever we are in the world. We could be on the dark side of the moon and still be just as close to the presence of God. There is nowhere we can go away from His indwelling presence. Moreover, as Spirit-baptized Christians we are imparted with special gifts to build up the body of Christ here on earth. Every Christian has at least one spiritual gift (Eph. 4:11). Paul tells us in Ephesians 4:7, "But grace was given to each one of us according to the measure of Christ's gift." Christ has honored us with these spiritual gifts.

This leads us to ask ourselves two questions. First, are we living our lives yielded to the Holy Spirit's power? Paul says in Ephesians 5:18, "Do not get drunk with wine . . . , but be filled with the Spirit." Are we yielding to His presence and His work by walking in obedience to the Word of God? When we obey the Lord's will, we are yielding our lives to be used by the Holy Spirit's power. Second, are we endeavoring to use our spiritual gifts in the life of the church? Church should not be merely for the believer to receive Christian teaching and participate in worship. Church must include the use of our gifts in the service of the body to build one another up (see Rom. 12; 1 Cor. 12; Eph. 4). To whom much is given, much is required. And the new covenant believer has been given a great honor by being baptized in the Holy Spirit.

The Honor of the Resurrection Body

The final honor we'll look at is the honor of receiving a *resurrection body* on the last day. This is the great hope that we look forward to. It means that death is not the end to our existence. A resurrection body that resembles Christ's resurrection body will be given to each of us at the Lord's return (1 Cor. 15:23). Until that day, our souls will be with the Lord in heaven after death. Then we will return to earth in spirit with the Lord to be reunited with our new bodies (1 Thess. 3:13; 4:14). Until then, the Christian's body will be "asleep" in the ground, awaiting the last day (4:15). But when the Lord returns, the Christian's body will be raised and the soul will be reunited with the new resurrection body, fitted for the new heavens and the new earth.

This resurrection body will be an upgraded version of the Christian's current body. It will not be subject to sin, decay, or death. As Paul puts it: "So it is with the resurrection of the dead. What is sown is perishable; what is raised is imperishable. It is sown in dishonor; it is raised in glory. It is sown in weakness; it is raised in power. It is sown a natural body; it is raised a spiritual body" (1 Cor. 15:42–44). Why does this matter? Because we know how things will end for us, we do not have to doubt our future existence. Whether death is a year from now, five years from now, or seventy years from now, our souls will immediately be with the Lord and our bodies will ultimately be raised anew. Therefore, Christians live in the knowledge that "to live is Christ, and to die is gain" (Phil. 1:21). Our future is fixed and secure. We will reign with Christ forever in renewed bodies. To be sure, we deserve to remain as dust (see Ps. 90). But God bestows on us the honor of going from dust to glory.

It's important that we understand these honors that we've been given. Some believers struggle in the Christian life simply because they are not aware of the honors that have been bestowed on them in Christ. We must go not to the world to understand our worth, but to Scripture. Every Christian is a saint, a friend of God, a child of God, baptized in the Holy Spirit, and promised a resurrection body. What amazing honors have been given to us in Christ! "For from his fullness we have all received, grace upon grace" (John 1:16). Much of what is needed in the Christian life is found by simply remembering who we are in Christ. In Christ, we are the recipients of the gifts of Christ (Eph. 4:8). We have not earned these honors. Rather, we are honored because of what Christ has done. It is all of grace. Therefore, ultimately all the honor goes to Him.

Worshiping
a Weighty God

One aspect of my upbringing that I'm thankful for is the emphasis on *all* of life as worship to God. Unfortunately, what I was taught often stopped there. Something was missing in the discussion, and this missing piece is the most important activity that we will ever do: engaging in *corporate worship*. Yes, all of life is worship. But there is something very important about the public honoring of God in corporate worship.

One of the great problems in the broader evangelical church is that few talk about a theology of corporate worship. We talk about singing and songs. We talk about preaching and the sermon. We talk about aspects of worship. But we often fail to appreciate and think about corporate worship itself as we should: its importance in our lives, its influence in our sanctification, the role it plays in motivating us to live the Christian life, and the honor it brings to a holy God. Fundamentally, this vertical aspect of corporate worship is what has been lost. Worship is first and foremost for God and not for us. Rather than understanding corporate worship primarily as something that God does for us, we should understand corporate worship as something that we give to God. The loss of this vertical meaning of corporate worship is reflected in how evangelicals now describe their corporate worship. The language of *worship service* has largely been abandoned for a myriad of other descriptors. But the word *service* reminds us that corporate worship is not primarily about us but about Him. Perhaps that does not seem as inviting or seeker-friendly in our secular culture, but I am convinced that many of the problems in the evangelical church stem from the fact that we have lost the real purpose of corporate worship.

This problem can even be seen in the "Navigator wheel." I was once talking to a well-known older pastor in Texas whom I greatly respect, and it so happened that he loved using the Navigator wheel in discipleship. During our conversation, I mentioned that the wheel had a serious deficiency, and he gave me a concerned, disapproving glance. I explained that there was a missing spoke on the wheel. The four spokes were *Scripture, prayer, fellowship,* and *evangelism*. But the wheel should contain five spokes, I said. *Corporate worship* is missing from the wheel. Jesus taught the disciples to worship God corporately, both in the synagogue and in Jerusalem at the feasts in the temple. This emphasis on corporate worship is seen in all of the Apostles' instructions about Christian discipleship. The pastor's response to my statement was that "corporate worship is implied on the wheel." In response, I said, "What is implied is soon to be forgotten." And indeed it has been, even though it remains one of the most important aspects of discipleship.

Dr. D. Martyn Lloyd-Jones often counseled those who were battling depression or other ailments to remain faithful in attending corporate worship. Lloyd-Jones believed that most Christians struggled with a lack of biblical doctrine and that this deficiency was the source of their spiritual problems. God uses corporate worship to bring us into contact with His Word in a unique way. Lloyd-Jones believed that preaching was the most important aspect in counseling.[1] No wonder the psalmist says, "I was glad when they said to me, 'Let us go to the house of the LORD!'" (Ps. 122:1). Are we "glad" when we wake up on the Lord's Day to go and worship Christ? That is a mark of a true Christian. We long for and love corporate worship. This desire is something that the Holy Spirit develops in our hearts. It is a fruit of the new birth. He gives us a heart for God.

When I was six or seven years old, I did not love coming to church. I didn't love listening to the sermons and singing the hymns. My mind was filled with daydreams of what I would play after the service ended. One Sunday during a family vacation in Wisconsin, we visited a church for Sunday worship in the little town of Cable. I did not want to be there. I wanted to be out on the lake, fishing. When the minister got up to preach, I excused myself to go to the bathroom to kill time. I walked into the foyer, and then down some stairs into the basement where the bathrooms were located. When I got to the basement, the thought came to me that the longer I could play in the basement, the less time I would need to be in the service. So I just started exploring the basement—opening up doors and looking into different classrooms. After looking into every room, I saw a stairwell going up to a door. I was curious. Perhaps those steps led to a gymnasium or to a playground outside. And so I went up the steps, opened the door, and boldly took three steps forward. I found myself right on the platform behind the preacher!

Everything stopped. The preacher paused and turned around to face me. I will never forget what he said: "Can I help you, young man?" Embarrassed, I mumbled, "No, sir, you cannot." And I did a hurried about-face and quickly jumped through the door from which I had come, to the sound of howling laughter behind me!

Needless to say, that incident marked my preconversion state. I viewed the worship of God as boring and redundant, something to be avoided rather than cherished. But now, there is nothing I desire more than to worship with God's people and sit under the powerful preaching of the Word of God.

God desires that we would yearn to worship with His people, and it is crucial that we learn how to honor God through corporate worship. The Scriptures speak of the importance of corporate worship over and over again. Let's examine eight truths about corporate worship.

The Old Testament Saints Worshiped Corporately

First, the Old Testament saints worshiped God corporately. This might seem like an obvious statement, but that is what the tabernacle and the temple were for. That is what the Psalter is for: the Psalms were the hymnbook of the Old Testament people of God. When they gathered at the temple, they would sing the Psalms. That's why many begin with the inscription, "To the choirmaster." David writes in Psalm 22:25, "From you comes my praise in the great congregation; my vows I will perform before those who fear him." In Psalm 35:18, he declares, "I will thank you in the great congregation; in the mighty throng I will praise you." The Psalms of Ascents (Pss. 120–134) were sung by the people of God as they traveled together on the road to Jerusalem. True Christianity has always been corporate.

Judaism and then Christianity were the only religions in the ancient world to worship God corporately. All the other religions featured individual worship but not gathered corporate worship. People would go up a hill and pray to their pagan deity, perhaps engaging in ecstatic utterances with others, but only Judaism was a corporate religion, gathering all its adherents to the temple to praise God together. Christianity continued as a corporate religion. Islam later copied Christianity, as did the Jehovah's Witnesses and the Mormon church. All cults copied the true Christian church's corporate worship.

Though the false religions and cults have mimicked Christianity's corporate nature, they do not understand the substance of why we worship corporately. The true people of God have always worshiped corporately because we are the only people in covenant with God. In the Old Testament, the people of God (since Adam) were always under the overarching covenant of grace. We are all saved by grace through faith. Through the mercy of God, individuals were brought into the family of God. We, as the church, have entered into the new covenant (Jer. 31; Ezek. 16). We are the new covenant people of God. It is a covenant that we enter into as individuals, but the covenant brings us into relationship with others who are also in covenant with God through Christ in faith.

Jesus Modeled Corporate Worship

Second, Jesus made corporate worship a priority in His life. When He was twelve years old, He attended the Passover feast in Jerusalem with His family. His parents left Jerusalem and began their return to Nazareth. When they finally realized that Jesus was not in their party, they returned to Jerusalem and searched for three days. Where did they find Him? In the temple. When His parents asked Him why He was in the temple, He said in Luke 2:49: "Why were you looking for me? Did you not know that I must be in my Father's house?" In other words: "Did you not realize that I would be communing with My Father with the people of God in the temple? You should have known where to find Me."

Jesus was passionately concerned about the public worship of God. He began His public ministry by cleansing the temple in Jerusalem because He saw that the Court of the Gentiles was being desecrated with animal vendors and money-changers. The public worship of God was made a mockery by the moneymaking schemes of the Sadducees. After He poured out the coins of the money-changers and freed the animals, He was asked why He had done such a thing. He simply responded, "Take these things away; do not make my Father's house a house of trade" (John 2:16). He did exactly the same thing at the end of His ministry (see Matt. 21; Mark 11; Luke 19).

Jesus dedicated Himself to honoring the corporate worship of God. This is why He brought His disciples to Jerusalem for the feasts. When we read the Gospels carefully, we notice that Jesus honored the three major feasts in Jerusalem: the Passover, the Feast of Weeks, and the Feast of Tabernacles (or Booths). He modeled, throughout His entire life, the importance of corporate worship with the people of God.

Jesus Taught the Necessity of Corporate Worship

Not only did Jesus model corporate worship, He also taught the importance of right corporate worship. His conversation with the woman at the well at the Samaritan village of Sychar hinged on the nature of corporate worship. Jesus asked the woman to fetch her husband, and she responded by admitting, "I have no husband" (John 4:17). Jesus then said to her: "You are right in saying, 'I have no husband'; for you have had five husbands, and the one you now have is not your husband. What you have said is true" (vv. 17–18). Jesus essentially pointed out her sin, saying: "This is why you are empty. This is why you are stumbling. This is why you are alienated from God." In response, "the woman said to him, 'Sir, I perceive that you are a prophet'" (v. 19).

Now that she knew who she was dealing with, she shifted the conversation to a debate over corporate worship. She said, "Our fathers worshiped on this mountain [Mount Gerizim], but you say that in Jerusalem is the place where people ought to worship" (v. 20). The Samaritans were the half-breed remnant of the northern ten tribes of Israel. To avoid mingling with Judah and going to Jerusalem, their ancestors had established other places of corporate worship rather than Jerusalem. Eventually the location of worship became Mount Gerizim in the north. So the Samaritan woman was asking Jesus to adjudicate the old debate between the Jews and the Samaritans over the location of corporate worship.

Jesus' response is astounding. "Jesus said to her, 'Woman, believe me, the hour is coming when neither on this mountain nor in Jerusalem will you worship the Father'" (John 4:21). A time was coming when worship would not be constrained by a specific location. Jesus then told her that the Samaritans actually worshiped in ignorance because they had not received the entire Old Testament as authoritative Scripture (since much of the Old Testament confirmed Jerusalem as the place of worship). "You worship what you do not know; we worship what we know, for salvation is from the Jews" (v. 22). The Samaritans did not worship God properly because they worshiped outside divine revelation.

We could say the same about much of the modern church's worship, which has hidden the Scriptures and embarked on practices and ideas that are found nowhere in Scripture. Sermons often consist of extended comedic stories with little or no Scripture mentioned. Songs have emotive chord structures but floundering, man-centered lyrics. Corporate prayers, if made at all, are often myopic and self-focused. We are a generation that worships a God whom we do not know in ways that God has not required. When Christmas Day has fallen on a Sunday, many evangelical churches have simply canceled their Sunday worship services. If we want to know why the Western church is often powerless and anemic, we must look no further than its corporate worship (or its lack thereof). When we are biblically illiterate in our approach, our corporate worship is, as Jesus observed, a "worship [of] what [we] do not know" (John 4:22).

Accompanying Jesus' rebuke of a failure to worship God properly according to Scripture was a radical transformation of corporate worship. No longer would a pilgrimage to Jerusalem be needed. Jesus declared: "But the hour is coming, and is now here, when the true worshipers will worship the Father in spirit and truth, for the Father is seeking such people to worship him. God is spirit, and those who worship him must worship in spirit and truth" (John 4:23–24). Jesus taught that the transformation would take place in this way: true worship would occur wherever God's people gather and worship in "spirit" and in "truth." By "spirit," He was saying that it's not enough to worship God externally and go through the motions. Worship must be from the heart. Mere outward religiosity is unacceptable to God.

The only way that we can offer up true worship from the heart is to be born again through the gospel. David prays in Psalm 51:16–17: "For you will not delight in sacrifice, or I would give it; you will not be pleased with a burnt offering. The sacrifices of God are a broken spirit; a broken and contrite heart, O God, you will not despise." No true worship can bypass the heart, and no true worship can bypass Christ and His atonement. We must be transformed from the inside out, in the heart, by Christ's blood in order to offer true worship to God.

By "truth," Jesus meant that we must worship God as He has actually revealed Himself to be. Of course, the Lord Jesus is the full disclosure of God. He is the Word made flesh who dwelt among us (John 1:14). He is the ultimate revelation of God—so much so that Jesus said that He is "the truth" (14:6). God has revealed Himself through His written Word and through His incarnate Word, His Son. We must worship God in the truth. To do so, we must go back to the Bible and ask: "Who is God? Who has He revealed Himself to be? And how does that affect our corporate worship?" There is no need to go to Jerusalem, but there is a great need to worship God from the heart and to worship Him as He really is.

The New Testament Church Corporately Worshiped

The New Testament church continued what had been modeled in the Old Testament and taught by Jesus regarding corporate worship. The Greek word for *church* is *ekklēsia*, which means "assembly." The church is made up of those who are called out together from the world. Christ died that we might come together as an assembly. Jesus told Peter, "You are Peter, and on this rock I will build my church [assembly]" (Matt. 16:18). Paul says in Ephesians 5:25, "Husbands, love your wives, as Christ loved the church and gave himself up for her." Christ died for the church—the called-out ones.

We see the early church come together corporately to worship. Luke records in Acts 2:42, "And they devoted themselves to the apostles' teaching and the fellowship, to the breaking of bread and the prayers." Where and how did this occur? Luke tells us four verses later: "And day by day, attending the temple together and breaking bread in their homes, they received their food with glad and generous hearts, praising God and having favor with all the people. And the Lord added to their number day by day those who were being saved" (Acts 2:46–47). The people gathered together in the temple and in their homes. The writer of Hebrews says, "I will tell of your name to my brothers; in the midst of the congregation I will sing your praise" (Heb. 2:12). Gathering together for corporate worship continued to be the general pattern for the early church.

The Apostles Taught Us to Corporately Worship

Not only did the Apostolic church model corporate worship, but the Apostles gave explicit instructions on how we are to worship our triune God. One of the foremost experts on New Testament worship is Dr. Terry Johnson, the longtime pastor of Independent Presbyterian Church in Savannah, Ga. Once during a visit to Savannah, I had the privilege of eating lunch with Dr. Johnson. Over the course of the meal, I asked him to explain the Apostles' teaching on corporate worship. His response was simple but insightful: "You do what the New Testament says!" And then after a long pause, he said: "You do only what the New Testament says! You go back and look at what the Apostles taught about corporate worship, and you do those things and only those things." If we look at the Apostles' teaching on corporate worship, we find five main practices that should make up our corporate worship, and all those things involve the Word of God.[2]

First, we are to *pray the Word of God*. We see this in Acts 2:42: "And they devoted themselves to . . . the prayers." Paul charges Timothy in 1 Timothy 2:1–2 along these lines: "First of all, then, I urge that supplications, prayers, intercessions, and thanksgivings be made for all people, for kings and all who are in high positions, that we may lead a peaceful and quiet life, godly and dignified in every way." When we come together, we are to pray not just for our congregational needs, but for the kingdom of God to advance. We are to plead with God for His mercy on our congregation and that we would be effective witnesses for the kingdom.

Dr. D. Martyn Lloyd-Jones said: "Prayer is always a great feature of every revival. Great prayer meetings, intercession, hour after hour. They pray for these people by name, lost people, and they plead, and they will not let God go, as it were. They are intent on this with a strange urgency."[3] So the church must be urgent in its prayers. The reason that many churches do not see conversions, changed lives, and the gospel advancing is that they do not pray corporately. They do not plead for the power of God, so they have no power. They do not plead for conversions, so they have no conversions. We must be urgent in our public prayers.

Second, we are to *sing the Word of God*. We sing psalms, hymns, and spiritual songs that reflect the truth of God's Word. When was the last time you turned on the radio and heard a Scientology song? Or a Hindu hymn? We don't hear them because such religions are not corporate in their worship. But because Christianity has always been corporate in its worship, the church has sung praises to God from the very beginning. Paul instructs us in Colossians 3:16, "Let the word of Christ dwell in you richly, teaching and admonishing one another in all wisdom, singing psalms and hymns and spiritual songs, with thankfulness in your hearts to God." He says in Ephesians 5:19 that we are to be "addressing one another in psalms and hymns and spiritual songs, singing and making melody to the Lord with your heart." We sing because we are a corporate people. And we are to sing Scripture and those songs and hymns that most closely reflect the doctrine and teaching of the Word of God.

Third, we are instructed to *read the Word of God*. Paul urges in 1 Timothy 4:13, "Until I come, devote yourself to the public reading of Scripture." Despite the simplicity of this practice, many churches have concluded that people would become bored with public Scripture reading, so they stopped doing it. But the Word of God is where the power is. The Holy Spirit dynamically uses the public reading of the Word of God in powerful ways in people's lives. It is the most basic and fundamental aspect of corporate worship and the foundation of our worship. Modern people may be tempted to think that singing is foundational, but it is secondary. Reading the Word of God is primary. When churches read Scripture, God speaks directly to His people through the reading of His Word.

Fourth, we are to *preach the Word of God.* In 2 Timothy 4:2, Paul exhorts Timothy to "preach the word; be ready in season and out of season; reprove, rebuke, and exhort, with complete patience and teaching." Preaching involves the explanation of God's Word so that the people can understand its meaning and its application. The purpose of preaching is ultimately that the hearers would exhibit Christlikeness for God's glory—that God's people would be more conformed to the image of Christ so that God will be magnified in their lives. The preacher is to proclaim the excellencies of Christ throughout all the Scriptures so that everyone may be presented "mature in Christ" (Col. 1:28). When we walk in maturity and obedience, God is honored. The preacher plays an important role in bringing God's people to honor Him.

Fifth, we are to *see the Word of God* visually depicted in the ordinances of the Lord's Supper and baptism. Our Lord Himself gave us these ordinances at the Last Supper and in the Great Commission (see Matt. 26:26–29; 28:19–20; Mark 14:22–25; Luke 22:18–20). Baptism visually depicts our union with Christ—that we are united by faith in His death, burial, and resurrection (Rom. 6:3–4; Col. 2:12). The Lord's Supper pictures Christ's substitutionary death for us (1 Cor. 11:26). In these glorious and God-given depictions of spiritual realities, God shows us through our physical senses what He has accomplished for us. As Dr. Sinclair Ferguson has said, "In the Lord's Supper we do not see a better Christ, but we do see Christ better." In his book *Devoted to God's Church*, he goes on to say that "what happens at the Table is a sermon. It is a proclamation of Jesus Christ crucified for our sins, raised again to be with us as our Lord, Saviour, Host and Friend."[4] The Holy Spirit powerfully uses these ordinances to strengthen the faith of the corporate body. Even though Christ is not physically present in the elements of the Lord's Supper or in the waters of baptism, a spiritual "participation" takes place with the risen Christ. Paul writes: "The cup of blessing that we bless, is it not a participation in the blood of Christ? The bread that we break, is it not a participation in the body of Christ?" (1 Cor. 10:16).

These are the five main elements that the Apostles taught are to be a part of our worship: praying the Word, singing the Word, reading the Word, preaching the Word, and seeing the Word. But what has happened over two thousand years is that the church has added elements to and subtracted elements from its worship. On one hand, the church said: "It's not enough. We need to add more. We need icons to pray to. We need theatrical depictions of the biblical stories. We need an element of entertainment." On the other hand, there has also been the idea that what the Apostles taught is unneeded: "Scripture readings lull people to sleep. True preaching will offend the seeker. The Lord's Supper, rightly administered, will make people uncomfortable." Over time, our corporate worship has become frightfully distorted. But as Dr. Johnson said to me that day, there is nothing we need to add to what the Apostles taught and nothing that we need to take away. God's Word is wonderfully sufficient.

Corporate Worship Demonstrates the Weightiness of God

One of the truths that the Bible teaches over and over again is that corporate worship demonstrates the weightiness of God. When we worship with God's people, the reality of who God is weighs so heavy on our hearts that it overflows corporately in a rush of praise and rejoicing. That is why corporate worship is so powerful. It is the collective statement that God is worthy of worship. This was Isaiah's experience when he glimpsed the heavenly throng worshiping God in the throne room.

Isaiah began by describing the year, saying, "In the year that King Uzziah died" (Isa. 6:1). King Uzziah was a very influential figure, and his death (around 740 BC) would have affected the people of his day in the same way that George Washington's death would have affected the young nation of America. It would have been a sad and ominous day. In this moment when everything was in turmoil and Israel seemed to be hopelessly thrown down, Isaiah said, "I saw the Lord sitting upon a throne" (v. 1). In other words, God was continuing to reign when everything was in upheaval. When everything seems hopeless, God is still reigning on His throne, "high and lifted up; and the train of his robe filled the temple" (v. 1).

Isaiah then described the picture: "Above him stood the seraphim. Each had six wings: with two he covered his face, and with two he covered his feet, and with two he flew. And one called to another and said: 'Holy, holy, holy is the LORD of hosts; the whole earth is full of his glory!'" (vv. 2–3). Dr. R.C. Sproul was famous for preaching on this passage. He expounds much on this scene in his book *The Holiness of God*. One fact that Dr. Sproul always used to remind people of is that only one attribute of God in the entirety of Scripture is ever repeated three times for emphasis: God's holiness.[5] It is repeated to put God's holiness in the superlative, to emphasize its all-encompassing nature.

The term *holy* means "separate." While we are made in God's image, God is separate from us in important ways. God is Creator, and we are His creatures. God is morally pure, and we are impure in our sin. In a sense, God's holiness is the sum of all His other attributes. He is separate and distinct from us by necessity of who He is. And for that reason, the angels declared that "the whole earth is full of his glory!" (v. 3). The word that is translated into English as "glory" is the same word often translated as "honor." It is the Hebrew word *kabod*. As we have seen, this word literally describes the weightiness of God. The whole earth reflects the weightiness of God. The whole earth proclaims the grandeur of God. When we look at a beautiful canyon, a glimmering sunset at the beach, or towering oaks covering a meadow, we are meant to feel the *kabod* of God, the heaviness of God.

After Isaiah heard these heaven-shaking words of the seraphim, he lamented: "'Woe is me! For I am lost; for I am a man of unclean lips, and I dwell in the midst of a people of unclean lips; for my eyes have seen the King, the LORD of hosts!' Then one of the seraphim flew to me, having in his hand a burning coal that he had taken with tongs from the altar. And he touched my mouth and said: 'Behold, this has touched your lips; your guilt is taken away, and your sin atoned for'" (vv. 5–7). This is the vision of God in heaven and a glimpse of the corporate worship in heaven. Not only was this worship taking place in Isaiah's day, it is taking place in ours as well. In the heavenly throne room of God, God is constantly being praised and honored.

This means that in a very real sense in our corporate worship, we are joining the heavenly throng. We gather with the people of God on earth and the people of God and the angels in heaven to declare that there is a thrice-holy God worthy of worship. We wonder why entire generations of young people are leaving the church. I believe it is because young people have never grasped the greatness of who God is. As fathers and mothers, if we want to establish our family in the Lord and want our children to fear God, we must make this public honoring of God a priority in our lives, and we must go to a church that prioritizes God-centered worship. To recalibrate our hearts to honor God, we must make God-centered worship primary in our lives.

J.B. Phillips wrote a book titled *Your God Is Too Small*. That title sums up the vision of most of the modern church: that God is still too small! When a huge vision of God is rediscovered, corporate worship will reflect that truth. Rather than being flippant and willy-nilly, it will resemble something much closer to Isaiah's vision. It will reflect the grandeur of God, the awe of God, and the fear of God. People will tremble as the Word is read and preached. They will see the greatness of the cross, where Christ died to reconcile them with a holy God. They will see the great honor of the Christian life and the privilege of being a child of God.

Moreover, our corporate worship is a witness to the world that there is a God in heaven worthy of honor. When people drive by a full church parking lot on Sunday mornings and evenings, they will be forced to reckon with the fact that there is a weighty God who is worthy of worship. The corporate worship of God proclaims to a lost world that our holy God is worthy of all worship and praise.

Our Souls Are Recalibrated in Corporate Worship

Seventh, God uses corporate worship to recalibrate our own souls. This is what the psalmist realizes in Psalm 73. Verse 1 is the thesis of the entire psalm: "Truly God is good to Israel, to those who are pure in heart." Do we believe that? It is easy to forget that God is sovereign and that He is good to His people. The psalmist's experience was that he saw the pagans who rejected God succeeding in life, and he saw himself struggling. He suffered while the pagans prospered. Therefore, it was difficult to reconcile God's promises to His people with his own experience. How often have we thought similar things? We become bogged down with the difficulties and frustrations of life, while it seems that the godless are winning every victory. How can God allow this to happen? The psalmist wonders whether his faithfulness has all been "in vain" (v. 13).

But then God brings the writer back to the right frame of mind. How does He do it? The psalmist reflects:

> But when I thought how to understand this,
>   it seemed to me a wearisome task,
> until I went into the sanctuary of God;
>   then I discerned their end.

> Truly you set them in slippery places;
>   you make them fall to ruin.
> How they are destroyed in a moment,
>   swept away utterly by terrors! (vv. 16–19)

It is in coming "into the sanctuary of God" that the psalmist regains a God-centered perspective (v. 17). It is in coming into the sanctuary that he is reminded of the futility of the godless life. It is in coming into the sanctuary that he remembers the wonder of enjoying the presence of God: "Nevertheless, I am continually with you; you hold my right hand" (v. 23). Then he pens these famous words:

> You guide me with your counsel,
>> and afterward you will receive me to glory.
> Whom have I in heaven but you?
>> And there is nothing on earth that I desire besides you.
> My flesh and my heart may fail,
>> but God is the strength of my heart and my portion forever.
>> (vv. 24–26)

By the end of the psalm, the psalmist has a completely different perspective. It is a complete 180-degree turn. He comes to the place where he realizes that all he truly needs is God. Terrible things may befall him, but they are nothing compared to the blessing he has in God. And it is the worship of God in the sanctuary that brings about this change in perspective.

The Future Is Corporate Worship

Not only does the Bible tell us that corporate worship is a priority in our earthly lives, but John says in Revelation 22 that corporate worship will define our existence in the new heavens and the new earth: "No longer will there be anything accursed, but the throne of God and of the Lamb will be in it, and his servants will worship him" (Rev. 22:3). History ends with the worship of God. We will gladly serve and rejoice in the Lord forever and ever. This is why God created us. If we love worship now, it will not compare to the bliss that we will experience forever in heaven as we give praise to God with His people from all ages past. What a glorious experience that will be.

God-centered worship forges God-centered Christians. Worship, which chiefly focuses on how the Bible informs us to worship God, will inevitably lead to corporate worship that truly honors Him. This not only forms people to see God as He really is—as holy. But it also proclaims to the world something important about the character of God. There is a holy God who is there, and He is worthy of all our worship. Our regular weekly participation in worship with God's people thus becomes a powerful testimony to a lost world that our triune God is worthy to be honored.

8

For the Sake
of the Name

Before our Lord ascended into heaven, He issued what is called the Great Commission, which contains the marching orders for the church:

> All authority in heaven and on earth has been given to me. Go therefore and make disciples of all nations, baptizing them in the name of the Father and of the Son and of the Holy Spirit, teaching them to observe all that I have commanded you. And behold, I am with you always, to the end of the age. (Matt. 28:18–20)

Let's consider a few observations that are important for us to understand.

First, notice the authority that Jesus claims. The Lord Jesus has fulfilled Psalm 2. He ascends to reign at the right hand of the Father, and He will reign until He puts all His enemies under

His feet (1 Cor. 15:25). The implication for us is clear. We do not send ourselves or speak on our own authority. Rather, we are commissioned by the Lord Jesus Himself, who is coming to judge the living and the dead. He is the One with the authority to command us to carry out this commission.

Second, notice the task itself: "Go therefore and make disciples." That word translated as "disciples" is *mathētēs* in Greek. It means "learner" or "follower," and it was used to describe the followers of the various rabbis in Israel. Each rabbi had his own followers, who learned to emulate the rabbi's teaching and life. Here, Jesus says that the scope of this disciple-making endeavor will be massive, extending to all nations. The Greek word for "nations," *ethnos*, doesn't merely denote geographic boundaries. Rather, it refers to people groups and language groups, as well as various nationalities. The mission is a global mission.

Third is the *how* of disciple-making. Jesus says that after someone professes faith in Him, the next step is to baptize the person. As we have seen, baptism is a sign and seal that outwardly marks someone as a follower of Christ. Baptism is Trinitarian in nature—we are baptized into "the name of the Father and of the Son and of the Holy Spirit" (Matt. 28:19). This is an outward step of obedience that every true disciple of Christ must take. I recall hearing the story of how Charles Spurgeon walked more than seven miles to be baptized in a river. He credited his baptism with "loosing his tongue to preach." It was a powerful testimony to both himself and others that he belonged to God. And so it is with every believer.

Unfortunately, many people stop at this point in the Great Commission, thinking that everything has been completed after converting and baptizing the nations. But this misses Jesus' next command: to teach "them to observe all that I have commanded you" (v. 20). Not only are we to teach new disciples the doctrines of Christianity, we are to teach them to obey the doctrines. Christian truth is always applicational and leads to life change. The Christian life is like the book of Ephesians—the first three chapters are doctrinal and the last three chapters are applicational. The doctrine and application are wedded together and cannot be separated. Christ's disciples must believe what He commanded and also obey what He commanded. Christlikeness is the ultimate mark of the true disciple of Jesus Christ.

Fourth, we must understand where the strength to carry out such a difficult endeavor comes from. Jesus promised in Matthew 28:20, "Behold, I am with you always, even to the end of the age." Jesus' presence and power through the ministry of the Holy Spirit enable us to carry out this commission. Without the Holy Spirit's powerful work, our efforts would be pointless. Salvation is of the Lord (Ps. 3:8; Jonah 2:9). Christ Himself must be the One who builds His church (Matt. 16:18).

Jesus says in Matthew 24:14: "This gospel of the kingdom will be proclaimed throughout the whole world as a testimony to all nations, and then the end will come." Before the Lord returns, the gospel will be proclaimed to all nations. And when this mission is finally completed, it will be marked by His bodily return. This is the task that Jesus gave His church to accomplish. We are not to be holy huddles, sequestered to ourselves. Rather, we are to reach the world for Christ and to be, in the words of Charles Spurgeon, "soul winners" and disciple makers. We are to take part in this glorious mission as the Holy Spirit has gifted us—as Bible teachers, as evangelists, as missionaries, or as what some call "rope holders."

A rope holder is someone who "holds the rope" for a missionary by funding the mission. Regardless of our particular role, we all have a part to play in this glorious mission that Christ has given us.

The First Great Missionary

The first great missionary was the Apostle Paul, missionary to the gentiles. We clearly see Paul's heart for the missionary task throughout Acts and Paul's epistles. In 1 Corinthians 9:19, he states, "For though I am free from all, I have made myself a servant to all." Literally, Paul says that he has made himself a *slave* (*doulos*) to all for the purpose "that I might win more of them." Notice this language of winning people. Paul is describing leading someone to Christ in terms of winning a victory.

This isn't a new concept in Scripture. Proverbs 11:30 notes, "The fruit of the righteous is a tree of life, and whoever captures souls is wise." Paul says, "To the Jews I became as a Jew, in order to win Jews" (1 Cor. 9:20). By this, he means that he followed the ceremonial laws when he was with Jews (even though they had been fulfilled in Christ) so that he might win the Jews to Christ. He was free from obeying those laws, but he observed them so that he could serve the Jews and keep an open door to the gospel.

Paul did the same with gentiles: "To those outside the law I became as one outside the law (not being outside the law of God but under the law of Christ) that I might win those outside the law" (v. 21). He is saying, in essence: "I put my own preferences aside in order that I might win people. Wherever I go, I try to relate to people the best way that I can in order that I might win them to Christ." Of course, disobeying the moral law of God was out of the question. That could never be compromised or disobeyed. Paul is simply referring to laying aside personal preferences to win people to Christ. In this way, Paul sought to carry out the Great Commission.

When Hudson Taylor went as a missionary to China, one of the groundbreaking things that he did was to discard his Western garb and instead wear the same clothing as the local people. This enabled him to be incredibly successful in reaching the Chinese people with the gospel. There are simple practices that we can adapt in order to reach our hearers, and the Apostle Paul was well aware of this. He became all things to all men, that he might win some (1 Cor. 9:22). He was willing to shelve his own rights so that he might reach both Jews and gentiles.

Paul understood his role in the missionary enterprise as that of an "ambassador." He says in 2 Corinthians 5:20: "Therefore, we are ambassadors for Christ, God making his appeal through us. We implore you on behalf of Christ, be reconciled to God." An ambassador is someone who is sent to speak on behalf of someone else as that person's representative. Paul understood himself to be an ambassador for Christ—proclaiming Christ on behalf of Christ. He says in Colossians 1:28–29, "Him we proclaim, warning everyone and teaching everyone with all wisdom, that we may present everyone mature in Christ. For this I toil, struggling with all his energy that he powerfully works within me." Is this our heart, to win people to Christ? Is this our struggle? Is this where we are putting all the energy that God gives us to advance Christ's mission in the world?

Paul's Motivation for Missions

What was Paul's motivation for missions? Clearly, he was greatly concerned about the lost and had a great passion for souls. But even the salvation of the lost was not his ultimate motivation. His highest motivation was the honor of God. He says in 2 Corinthians 4:15, "For it is all for your sake, so that as grace extends to more and more people it may increase thanksgiving, to the glory of God."

Notice in this verse first the burden for the lost—"For it is all for your sake." Certainly, Paul was motivated by the need of his fellow man. But that need was ultimately to lead to the increase of "thanksgiving, to the glory of God." That word "thanksgiving" is the Greek word *eucharisteō*, from which we get the English word *eucharist*. It means "to render thanks to God." In other words, Paul ministered the gospel so that worship would increase and God would be most glorified. Paul's great motivation was the *glory and honor of God*. Paul was a God-centered missionary who wanted other people to praise and worship the living Christ. He wanted God to receive the highest glory and heaviest honor. Paul explained at the beginning of his letter to the Romans that his missionary endeavor was all "for the sake of his name among all the nations" (Rom. 1:5).

Have you ever noticed all the doxological statements in Paul's writings? They are everywhere: "For from him and through him and to him are all things. To him be glory forever. Amen" (Rom. 11:36). "To the only wise God be glory forevermore through Jesus Christ! Amen" (16:27). "To the King of the ages, immortal, invisible, the only God, be honor and glory forever and ever. Amen" (1 Tim. 1:17). "To him be honor and eternal dominion. Amen" (6:16). "To this end we always pray for you, that our God may make you worthy of his calling and may fulfill every resolve for good and every work of faith by his power, so that the name of our Lord Jesus may be glorified in you, and you in him, according to the grace of our God and the Lord Jesus Christ" (2 Thess. 1:11–12). In 1 Corinthians 10:31, Paul says, "So, whether you eat or drink, or whatever you do, do all to the glory of God." Paul believed that the glory of God and the honor of His name were at the very center of his missionary efforts. God must be glorified. His name must be honored. Pagans must be turned into worshipers. There must be rejoicing in God's salvation for God's glory.

As a high school student, I was deeply affected by John Piper's book *Let the Nations Be Glad!* Growing up in the church and having gone on mission trips, I had a great heart for the lost, and I assumed that this was the highest end of missions: to save sinners. Piper, in very clear terms, pointed me even higher with his argument: "Missions exists because worship doesn't."[1] Yes, we want to see people saved, but the ultimate purpose in that is that they might become worshipers of the triune God, that God would receive the glory. Piper plainly states: "Missions is not God's ultimate goal. Worship is. And when this sinks into a person's heart, everything changes. The world is often turned on its head and everything looks different, including the missionary enterprise."[2]

Jesus' encounter with the woman at the well in John 4 is reminiscent of Piper's thesis. Jesus said, "The hour is coming, and is now here, when the true worshipers will worship the Father in spirit and truth, for the Father is seeking such people to worship him" (John 4:23). Notice the last part: "The Father is seeking such people to worship him." Jesus clearly had a big view of God. He knew the Father intimately and had been with the Father from the beginning. The Father was in Him and He was in the Father (14:11). Jesus knew that the Father's ultimate purpose for His incarnation, death, and resurrection was to create a throng of worshipers. In other words, the endgame of missions is worship.

Therefore, we must view missions in the way that God views missions. Like Jesus, we must have a big view of God, viewing our mission and our lives from a God-centered perspective. Because God desires the advance of His own name, we are to make that our desire as well as we carry the banner of the glory of God. God is exalting His name among the nations, and we as Christ's disciples must grasp the doxological end of our mission. It is this vision that will drive us to do difficult things. When we are driven by a desire for the glory of God and the honor of God's name, we will be able to endure when the moment of trial comes without giving up.

Endurance Needed

A God-centered vision of ministry enables us to endure to the end. This is something we must remember as hostility and animosity toward Christianity grows increasingly prevalent. If we are effective for the kingdom, we will be opposed by Satan and the world. We will need to "endure suffering," as Paul told Timothy (2 Tim. 4:5). Paul makes this statement about his own experience as a missionary in 2 Corinthians 4:8–12:

> We are afflicted in every way, but not crushed; perplexed, but not driven to despair; persecuted, but not forsaken; struck down, but not destroyed; always carrying in the body the death of Jesus, so that the life of Jesus may also be manifested in our bodies. For we who live are always being given over to death for Jesus' sake, so that the life of Jesus also may be manifested in our mortal flesh. So death is at work in us, but life in you.

Paul describes his affliction by using the word *thlibō*, which means "to be compressed in a tight space." When I think about this picture, I envision the original *Star Wars* movie when Han Solo, Princess Leia, Luke Skywalker, and Chewbacca jump into the giant trash compactor. The walls begin closing in to compress them. They would have been crushed had R2D2 not turned off the compactor from outside. This was the nature of Paul's missionary experience. The walls were closing in to crush him, but God's grace kept him from being destroyed.

A few verses later, Paul says that all this pain and difficulty is for the "sake" of the Corinthians (2 Cor. 4:15). Everything he endured was in the hope of showing the greatness of the gospel so that the Corinthians might believe, be saved, and glorify God. In fact, this is precisely what the Lord Jesus said would describe Paul's ministry. After Paul had been blinded on the Damascus road, Jesus told Ananias, "For I will show him how much he must suffer for the sake of [the] name" (Acts 9:16).

Suffering for the Sake of the Name

If we understand what Jesus and Paul are saying, we see that suffering and loss are what Christ ordained for His servants so that the gospel might go forth. The means of missions is the same as the end of missions. The end of missions is the honor of God's name, and the means of missions is the honor of God's name. And one of the chief ways that God shows the value of His name is through the suffering of His servants. When an evangelist endures persecution for the sake of the gospel, those he is trying to reach realize the weightiness of the evangelist's endeavor. "The name" of Christ is shown to be honored in our suffering, and as a result, the lost believe the gospel.

Therefore, one reason that Christians experience hardship and suffering is so that the world might see that there is a God in heaven worth honoring. Paul told the Philippians, "For it has been granted to you that for the sake of Christ you should not only believe in him but also suffer for his sake" (Phil. 1:29). God Himself had ordained the suffering of the Philippians, and their suffering would ultimately be a testimony to the greatness of God and the grandeur of the gospel.

This turns the "prosperity gospel" on its head. Not only does God not promise material prosperity in this life, He promises that there will be hardship and difficulty for those who desire to live godly lives. Therefore, Paul tells Timothy, "Indeed, all who desire to live a godly life in Christ Jesus will be persecuted" (2 Tim. 3:12). Peter ties this picture of suffering for Christ to the battle that we now wage against Satan and the dark realm: "Be sober-minded; be watchful. Your adversary the devil prowls around like a roaring lion, seeking someone to devour. Resist him, firm in your faith, knowing that the same kinds of suffering are being experienced by your brotherhood throughout the world" (1 Peter 5:8–9). The devil is attacking Christians across the whole world, and the result is "suffering."

The cross must always come before the crown in our lives. The crown awaits us in heaven, but as we follow Christ, it is the cross that we must carry now (Luke 9:23). This is what Jesus promised us. He told His disciples in the upper room: "Remember the word that I said to you: 'A servant is not greater than his master.' If they persecuted me, they will also persecute you. If they kept my word, they will also keep yours" (John 15:20). We must not expect to be treated better than our Lord. We will experience resistance, hardship, and persecution. That is why endurance is so greatly needed. Paul told Timothy, "Share in suffering as a good soldier of Christ Jesus" (2 Tim. 2:5). Part of being a soldier is enduring the difficulties of war: the elements, the hunger, the lack of sleep, the trauma of combat, the pain of wounds, and even death itself. In a similar vein, Paul teaches that as good Christian soldiers, we must be prepared to endure the onslaught that Satan will mount against us.

When Jonathan Edwards was ministering in Northampton, Mass., he housed a young missionary named David Brainerd. Brainerd, a famous Yale student, had said upon graduation, "I never, since I began to preach, could feel any freedom to 'enter into another man's labours', and settle down in the ministry where the gospel was preached before."[3] Brainerd would go on to serve at Stockbridge with the Kaunaumeek Indians. In Iain Murray's biography of Edwards, he records Brainerd as saying, "There appeared to be nothing of any considerable importance to me but holiness of heart and life, and the conversion of the heathen to God."[4] He labored tirelessly for several years, but by 1746, Brainerd had developed a serious case of tuberculosis, which severely hindered his work. He could hardly breathe without strain. He was nursed by Jerusha Edwards in Jonathan Edwards' home until he went to be with the Lord in 1747, at the age of twenty-nine. Years after his ministry and death, the Indians were visited with a great work of God in the summer of 1775.[5]

Suffering to Display God's Power

Why would God allow such a thing to happen to one of His great saints? When we experience great difficulty in our lives, we often ask the same question: "Why is God allowing me to endure this trial? this illness? this catastrophe?" Paul points out that we are "always carrying in the body the death of Jesus, so that the life of Jesus may also be manifested in our bodies" (2 Cor. 4:10). He is telling us that just as the Lord Jesus achieved our salvation—not by exercising strength but by suffering weakness on the cross—so we also reach the lost through our suffering. As we noted earlier, this shows the worthiness of God's name and manifests the greatness of His power in us.

Paul notes in the next verse: "For we who live are always being given over to death for Jesus' sake" (v. 11). Who is giving us over to death? God is. We are being given over to death for Jesus' sake, "so that the life of Jesus also may be manifested in our mortal flesh. So death is at work in us, but life in you" (vv. 11–12). What a remarkable statement. The Corinthians saw the resurrection life and power of Jesus manifested in the weakness and suffering of the Apostle. In other words, God's strength was most greatly seen in Paul's weakness and suffering.

The same is true for us. God's power is seen in our weakness and suffering. A few chapters later, Paul says: "For the sake of Christ, then, I am content with weaknesses, insults, hardships, persecutions, and calamities. For when I am weak, then I am strong" (2 Cor. 12:10). He is content to walk in weakness so that the gospel may be seen as great. His ultimate desire is to see the supernatural power of God displayed. As a result of this strength in weakness, God will receive all the honor from our ministry. God displays this power in "jars of clay" (4:7). We are simply the earthen vessels that God uses "to show that the surpassing power belongs to God and not to us." God uses weak men and women in His kingdom so that He and He alone will receive the glory.

In summary, the highest end of missions is the honor of God, and the means of carrying out that mission will be fraught with suffering and persecution. This suffering and persecution shows that Christ's name is worthy of suffering and that the power to carry out the mission belongs to God and not to us. We are simply "jars of clay" who receive the gift of participating in His glorious mission. What is needed from us is endurance. We must not be surprised when we face opposition and difficulty because that is God's design—that through suffering the world might see His greatness through us. And Christ Himself is our great example in this mission. The writer of Hebrews urges, "Consider him who endured from sinners such hostility against himself, so that you may not grow weary or fainthearted" (Heb. 12:3). If Jesus endured, we can also endure with His power. Jesus promised in the Great Commission that He is with us, even to the end of the age. He will carry us through, all the way to the end.

9

Give Honor to Whom Honor Is Due

When I was a series commander at Parris Island, I marched in every graduation parade at the end of the thirteen-week recruit training cycle. When each company graduated, several thousand family members and friends gathered from across the country to see their new Marines graduate from boot camp. Often, important dignitaries and military heroes would attend the parade. After one of the graduation parades that I had marched in, I was walking back to my office when another drill instructor approached me. He informed me that I had walked past a Medal of Honor recipient and had failed to give him a proper salute. (It is a rule that Medal of Honor recipients must be saluted by everyone in the military, regardless of rank.)

I explained to the drill instructor that I had not seen the Medal of Honor recipient. Desiring to not cause offense and to give proper honor to this man, I walked back to the parade grounds, found the Medal of Honor recipient, and gave him a salute. He saluted back and then shook my hand and profusely thanked me. This might sound silly to those who have not served in the military, but it is an important tradition. We must give honor to whom honor is due. Practices such as these sustain every institution and government. No institution can be maintained without honor being shown to those who have earned it.

God says the same thing regarding the institutions that He has established: the family, the civil government, and the church. In these institutions, we are to show honor to those to whom God has given leadership. This is one of the Christian's most basic obligations and responsibilities. All three of these spheres are under God's authority and have been established by Him through His Word, and all are ultimately regulated by His Word. We have a responsibility to obey our leaders in these spheres because God has instituted them.

The caveat, of course, is that we are to submit to each institution only insofar as we can do so according to the Word of God. That is an important concept because it means that no one's authority is unlimited. If someone tells us to do something that is contrary to the Word of God, then we must obey God rather than men (Acts 5:29). If our parents, the federal government, or the leadership of our church asks us to do something that violates the Word of God, then God's Word is to trump their authority. They too are underneath God and His Word.

That being said, one of the marks of a reverent Christian who lives for the honor of God is giving joyful obedience to governing authorities. When we obey these authorities, we are actually giving honor to God, who established them. Obedience becomes a very tangible and practical way for us to show the weightiness of God in our lives.

Honor in the Family

Paul commands children, "Honor your father and mother (this is the first commandment with a promise), that it may go well with you and that you may live long in the land" (Eph. 6:2–3). Children must "honor" their parents (the fifth of the Ten Commandments) by showing deference and obedience to them. Honor is shown through obedience. In fact, Paul says explicitly that children are to "obey [their] parents in the Lord" (v. 1). This is critically important because God has established the responsibility for parents to train and teach their children to know and fear God. Proverbs 1:8–9 urges, "Hear, my son, your father's instruction, and forsake not your mother's teaching, for they are a graceful garland for your head and pendants for your neck." Children are to honor and revere their parents, and in so doing learn how to honor and fear God. It is the ungodly and lawless, Paul notes, who attack and dishonor their parents (1 Tim. 1:9). There is a direct correlation between those who dishonor their parents and those who dishonor God.

Paul then points to the authority of the parents. "Fathers, do not provoke your children to anger, but bring them up in the discipline and instruction of the Lord" (Eph. 6:4). The relationship between parent and child is not a friend-to-friend relationship, though that certainly comes later as the child matures into adulthood. The relationship is one of submission and authority. The parents stand in the place of God to their children, exhorting them to obey the Lord's commands and honor Him with their lives.

This is why it's so important for parents to teach their children obedience. Ephesians 6:1 is the first verse that my wife and I had our children memorize. Early on, we taught them that obedience consists of three things: (1) the obedience must be *immediate*; (2) the obedience must be *complete*; and (3) the obedience must be *cheerful*. Put negatively, obedience must not be neglected, it must not be halfway, and it must not be done in anger or bitterness. Children are to obey quickly, thoroughly, and with their whole heart. If any of these are neglected, children should be lovingly disciplined so that they will learn proper obedience. This might sound harsh in today's culture. In actuality, it is one of the kindest things you can do for your children because you are establishing them on the path of wisdom. You are teaching them to fear the Lord.

When children reach adulthood, they are to establish their own families and are no longer to be under the authority of their parents. Therefore, the command to obey parents applies when a child lives as a dependent in the parents' household. But as adults, we still strive to honor our parents as we are able. Recently I was talking to my uncle, a successful businessman in San Antonio. He related a story to me about an interaction between him and my grandpa, Charles Castleberry, on the way to church. My uncle serves in leadership as a deacon at his church, and my grandpa, who was visiting, was attending church with him. My grandfather had served as an infantry officer in the Marine Corps and ran his own real estate business for fifty years. He also taught a televised Sunday school class for more than forty years at the First Baptist Church of Lake Jackson, Texas. On this particular morning, my uncle came out to his truck without wearing his usual tie. When my grandfather saw him, he said, "Keary, are you serving as a deacon at your church?" My uncle replied, "Yes, sir, I am." He then said, "Then, Keary, why are you not dressed like a deacon?" I myself have had many similar encounters with my grandfather, which is, I am sure, part of the reason that I preach in a coat and tie to this day! I asked my uncle how he had responded. My uncle said: "Well, I went back into the house and put on a tie! It is not as big a deal to me, but I wanted to honor my dad." That is exactly the right idea. As much as we can, in the Lord, we desire to honor our parents.

Honoring Parents as the Foundation to Honoring God

Parental relationships stay with us throughout our lives. When Jesus was hanging on the cross, one of the most important provisions He made before His death was to place His mother, Mary, in the care of the Apostle John (John 19:26). Paul would go on to teach, "If a widow has children or grandchildren, let them first learn to show godliness to their own household and to make some return to their parents, for this is pleasing in the sight of God" (1 Tim. 5:4). Paul expected children to provide and care for their aging parents.

Our Lord took this responsibility very seriously, and He condemned the religious leaders of the day for neglecting their own parents. In Mark 7, a question arose about hand-washing. The scribes and Pharisees had instituted a policy in which people had to wash their hands ceremonially before and after they ate, even though the Old Testament law prescribed that only the priests needed to do this (Ex. 30:18). The Jewish leaders asked Jesus, "Why do your disciples not walk according to the tradition of the elders, but eat with defiled hands?" (Mark 7:5). The charge was that Jesus and the disciples did not keep the Pharisees' tradition, which had added requirements to the law of God.

Jesus rebuked them for their hypocrisy of neglecting God's law while "teaching as doctrines the commandments of men" (v. 7).

Not only had they added to God's Word, but they had neglected God's Word. They had substituted their own religion in place of the Word of God. Which specific law had they broken? The fifth commandment. Jesus admonished them:

> "You have a fine way of rejecting the commandment of God in order to establish your tradition! For Moses said, 'Honor your father and your mother'; and, 'Whoever reviles father or mother must surely die.' But you say, 'If a man tells his father or his mother, "Whatever you would have gained from me is Corban"' (that is, given to God)—then you no longer permit him to do anything for his father or mother, thus making void the word of God by your tradition that you have handed down. And many such things you do." (Mark 7:9–13)

Essentially, Jesus was accusing the Pharisees of encouraging people to give money to the temple, even though they should have given these funds to support their parents. Rather than honoring their aging fathers and mothers, which the law of God commanded, the religious leaders wanted to appropriate the people's money for themselves.

Why did Jesus make such a big deal out of this neglect? The fifth commandment is important because it is the link between the first four and the final five commands. The first four are about our relationship with God—"You shall have no other gods before me," "You shall not make for yourself a carved image," "You shall not take the name of the LORD your God in vain," and "Remember the Sabbath day, to keep it holy" (Ex. 20:3–4, 7–8). These commands are all vertical. They deal with man's relationship to God.

The final five commands deal with man's relationship to his fellow man. Coming between these two groups is the commandment to "honor your father and your mother" (v. 12). I think God placed this command here because when children learn to honor their father and mother, they are learning both to honor God and how to love their fellow man. Parents were instructed to teach their children how to honor and fear God (Deut. 6:7). This helps us understand why the promise was given that they would live "long in the land" (Ex. 20:12). The promise was given not merely so that children would be nice to their parents. The promise was given because it assumed that if children honored their father and mother, they would also honor God. And if they honored God, then they would live long in the land.

Similarly, learning to honor our parents is the key to learning how to honor our fellow man. Children who learn to honor their father and mother will also understand the respect that is to be given to their fellow man, as seen in the last five commands. In this way, the path of enduring faithfulness for a people runs through the fifth commandment. The nation that has children who honor their parents puts itself in the path of God's blessing. The nation that has children who honor their parents tends toward peace and prosperity. This is why Jesus so adamantly emphasized it. The Pharisees had eroded the entire foundation for the honor of God in their culture. Jesus emphasized that for it to be recovered, they had to go back to the basics—to the fifth commandment.

Honoring Governing Authorities

We must understand the importance of honoring the governing authorities that God has placed over us. This is especially important to understand in light of government overreach and increasing totalitarianism on the part of secular authorities. Paul addresses this issue in Romans 13. He commands, "Pay to all what is owed to them: taxes to whom taxes are owed, revenue to whom revenue is owed, respect to whom respect is owed, honor to whom honor is owed" (Rom. 13:7). Christians are to give basic honor and respect to the leaders who are placed over us. We need to remember this, especially when we are increasingly under leaders with whom we do not agree. We are to give a certain respect and honor because of the office that a person holds.

In the military, if a high-ranking officer comes into a room, the person closest to the door will call out, "Attention on deck." At that point, everybody stands up and assumes the position of attention, regardless of whether they happen to like that officer. Attention is called because of the rank that the officer holds. Likewise, one salutes when passing a higher-ranking officer. In so doing, the rank and office held by that individual is being saluted. This is the idea that Paul is communicating—there is a God-given honor and decorum that comes with the office being held by an individual.

There is also a God-given authority for the government to promote good and punish evil. Paul says explicitly, "For there is no authority except from God, and those that exist have been instituted by God" (Rom. 13:1). Those of us in the Reformed faith hold to the doctrine of divine providence, which says that every event and outcome is ultimately a result of God's sovereign will (though God is not the author of evil and does not cause people to sin). In that light, we must understand every governing authority as one whom God has placed in that position. Paul's conclusion, then, is: "Therefore whoever resists the authorities resists what God has appointed, and those who resist will incur judgment" (v. 2).

The next verse is important because it qualifies the authority that government leaders possess. Do government leaders have complete authority over our lives? For example, are they allowed to mandate that everyone wear pink shirts? Of course not. Paul gives a much narrower sphere of authority to governing leaders: "For rulers are not a terror to good conduct, but to bad. Would you have no fear of the one who is in authority? Then do what is good, and you will receive his approval" (v. 3). God's expectation is that a ruler is to promote what is good according to God's law and to punish what is evil according to God's law.

The Puritan Samuel Rutherford reiterated this point in the book *Lex Rex*, which translated from Latin means "The Law Is King." The title itself communicates an important truth to remember. God's moral law is "king" over every government leader, whether he or she acknowledges it or not. As long as the leader governs in accordance with God's law, punishing evil and rewarding good, then we must and should cheerfully obey the leader. In fact, Paul points out that when the government leader rules in this way, he or she is God's "deacon" or "servant" (Rom. 13:4). The leader is carrying out God's design for civil justice. The leader's authority is to punish evil (as God defines it) and promote righteousness (as God defines it). But if a government leader says, as Nebuchadnezzar did, that we are to bow down to a statue, we must obey God rather than men. Our highest allegiance is to the Lord.

I believe that the coming years will see many more tests awaiting the church. As hearts grow cold and animosity builds, governing leaders will increasingly target Christian churches. In the face of this opposition, we must have spines of steel like John Bunyan, the author of *The Pilgrim's Progress*, who declared that he would rather be thrown in jail than to be restricted from preaching the gospel.[1]

America's founding fathers had the foresight to recognize that civil authorities would be tempted to overreach beyond their God-given jurisdiction. That is why they enacted what is called the Bill of Rights. The Bill of Rights lists certain rights possessed by citizens that cannot be infringed on by the government, such as the right of free speech, the right to bear arms, the right to personal property, the right to practice religion freely, and the freedom of the press. The founders were wise in delineating, in accordance with the principles of Romans 13, the limited sphere of influence that the government possesses.

In summary, we are to obey and submit to governing authorities as much as we can under the lordship of Jesus Christ. We also recognize the limited sphere of government—that it pertains to maintaining public justice and protection, not restricting individual liberties and the responsibilities that we have before God. Seen in this light, Paul's command to pray "for kings and all who are in high positions" becomes all the more meaningful (1 Tim. 2:2). Lord willing, government leaders will be converted, stay within their God-given jurisdictional sphere, and promote justice for all. When there is civil peace and order, the gospel has great opportunity for advancement. Yes, people are converted during times of persecution. But revival and awakening most often occur during times of civil peace and order, when the church is able to function freely in its proclamation of the gospel without restrictions.

Honoring Church Authorities

Honor is also to be given to church authorities, particularly to church elders. Paul notes, "Let the elders who rule well be considered worthy of double honor, especially those who labor in preaching and teaching" (1 Tim. 5:17). He explains in verse 18, "For the Scripture says, 'You shall not muzzle an ox when it treads out the grain,' and, 'The laborer deserves his wages.'" Paul teaches that the elders who minister the Word of God should be given respect and honor by their congregations (in the New Testament, the terms "elder," "bishop," and "pastor" are used interchangeably). This specifically includes financial support. These leaders are to be provided for with "double honor."

To illustrate the principle, the Apostle uses the example of an ox treading grain. Just as one should not muzzle an ox, which would prevent it from eating from the grain it treads, so the pastor/elder should not be denied the fruit that his ministry produces. I have heard congregations express the sentiment, "Lord, we will keep the minister poor, so that you can keep him humble." That grates against what Paul is saying. In fact, that view shows a lack of respect for the high responsibility of preaching and teaching the Word of God. The respect that is shown to faithful pastors directly represents our respect for God's Word and ultimately for God Himself.

It is interesting that Paul ties "double honor" to those who labor in the faithful teaching of the Word of God. The implication is that if a minister ceases to apply himself appropriately to the study of God's Word or departs from sound doctrine, then he is not deserving of "double honor." In this case, the minister's departure from sound doctrine would be disqualifying. The amount of honor given to a leader should be in accordance with his faithfulness to the Word of God.

The writer of Hebrews says something similar: "Remember your leaders, those who spoke to you the word of God. Consider the outcome of their way of life, and imitate their faith" (Heb. 13:7). It is the Word of God that is to be the instrument of the faithful pastor and elder. He is to preach the Word of God and live the Word of God. If an elder teaches something that is contradictory to sound doctrine, then we are to obey God rather than men. Moreover, similar to the limited sphere of the civil government's authority, the sphere of church authority is also limited.

Spiritual authority is related to the commands of the Word of God. No pastor, for example, has the authority to tell someone when to purchase property or a vehicle, change jobs, or the like. I have heard of churches that require their members to submit their family budgets to the church. That is not the church's jurisdiction; it is the individual's and the family's jurisdiction. Obviously, a pastor can give advice about job changes or big purchases, but these liberties would fall under decisions of individual conscience and, in the case of married couples, the family.

Elders have the authority to tell church members what God's Word says and, if necessary, point out when their lives are out of step with the truth. The writer of Hebrews goes on to say: "Obey your leaders and submit to them, for they are keeping watch over your souls, as those who will have to give an account. Let them do this with joy and not with groaning, for that would be of no advantage to you" (Heb. 13:17). In that regard, we have an important responsibility before God to "obey [our] leaders," but this must be on the basis of clear biblical truth rather than mere opinion.

To put it another way, the only authority that an elder has over his flock is the authority of God's Word. As a shepherd and watchman on the wall, the elder is to serve with an open Bible, exhorting and encouraging, teaching and preaching, admonishing and counseling. America is the land of cults and heretics, and many false teachers have led people astray under the guise of religious authority. Many have claimed, "God told me to do this." And subsequently, people who didn't know their Bibles followed them.

Conclusion

We are to honor family, government, and church authorities as much as we can under God. In so doing, we will give great honor to the Lord, and we will ensure that we preserve these institutions for our own good. Honoring people in these institutions might seem tangential to our focus on honoring God. But we must remember the doctrine of God's providence. God established the institutions of the family, civil government, and the church, and it is God who sovereignly places leaders in these institutions. Hearts that love to rebel against any and every authority over them are hearts that also rebel against God. Therefore, as God-centered Christians, we must lead by example in honoring all those whom God has placed in authority over us as much as we can under the ultimate lordship of Jesus Christ.

10

A Life Lived for God

Have you ever asked yourself the question, "What do I live for?" One of the most radical differences between Christianity and secular ideologies lies in the center of our motivations. The message of secular humanism is to live for yourself: follow your dreams, your heart, and your desires. I recently heard a world-famous celebrity say that she wanted to live for as long as she could while having as much pleasure as she could. That seems to be the prevailing worldview of our secular age. The Bible, however, asserts that we are to live for God. He is the center of our heart and desires. We are left in this world for one thing: His glory.

Paul says in 1 Corinthians 10:31 that "whether you eat or drink, or whatever you do, do all to the glory of God." He tells the church at Rome: "For from him and through him and to him are all things. To him be glory forever. Amen" (Rom. 11:36). He says in his letter to Timothy: "To him be honor and eternal dominion. Amen" (1 Tim. 6:16). One of the great Dutch theologians of the twentieth century, Herman Bavinck, observed, "The Christian moral life has faith as its root, the law as its rule, and the honor of God as its goal."[1]

As we have seen, the Christian stands before God on the basis of the work of Christ. Christ's honoring of God is credited to us through faith. Yet Paul's exhortation is that we are now to conduct ourselves in a "manner . . . worthy of the gospel of Christ" (Phil. 1:27). This work of honoring God in our lives is called *sanctification*. It is both a work of the Holy Spirit, pressing us forward to honor God, and our working in partnership with the Holy Spirit in striving to live for Christ (2:12–13).

Where are we to begin in this process? It is sometimes hard to know where to start, because so much material in the Bible addresses the Christian life. For example, we could start by looking at Jesus' instructions for His disciples in the Sermon on the Mount. We could start by looking at what David says in several psalms, particularly Psalms 1, 16, and 23. We could look at the virtues that Peter outlines in 2 Peter 1.

The Apostle Paul: A Case Study

In seeking to answer this question, we'll focus on a case study of the Apostle Paul, who took the gospel to the gentiles and himself exhorted believers to follow his example. He urged the Corinthians, "Be imitators of me, as I am of Christ" (1 Cor. 11:1). He told the Philippians, "Join in imitating me, and keep your eyes on those who walk according to the example you have in us" (Phil. 3:17). We learn by gaining knowledge, but in terms of growing in wisdom, it helps us tremendously to see the principles fleshed out and the truth embodied in a person.

Paul's Motivation

Perhaps no passage encapsulates Paul's passion and motivation for the Christian life like Philippians 1:20–21. It's a great starting point for understanding the heart of the Apostle Paul:

> It is my eager expectation and hope that I will not be at all ashamed, but that with full courage now as always Christ will be honored in my body, whether by life or by death. For to me to live is Christ, and to die is gain.

Notice Paul's words. His hope is that he will never be ashamed. "Ashamed of what?" we moderns might ask. Ashamed of *the cross*. As we have seen, the cross was an instrument of public shame. Paul said, "We preach Christ crucified, a stumbling block to Jews and folly to Gentiles" (1 Cor. 1:23). The idea that the Son of God could be crucified on a cross was the great stumbling block for many in the ancient world. But Paul, knowing the power of the cross, essentially says, "It's my expectation and hope that I will not be ashamed of the cross, but will preach it with courage." In so doing, he reveals his passion that Christ "will be honored" (Phil. 1:20)—regardless of what happens to him—both in life and in death.

The Greek word that is translated as "honor" here is *megalynō*. The prefix *mega* essentially means "to magnify" something. Paul is saying, "I want Christ to appear as big as He really is in my life by the way that I live." This is his objective. Moreover, in doing this, the Apostle proclaims that he has nothing to lose. He will make Christ appear weighty either in life or in death. Either way, Paul's objective will be accomplished and Christ will be honored. This is the mindset that propelled Paul to turn the world upside down. He was a man with a mission, nothing to lose, and everything to gain.

This is the singular focus that we must adopt. Our motivation must be to make Christ appear huge in our lives, to honor Him. The world is telling us that many other ideas and philosophies should energize us, but none of them compare with this. This passion propelled Paul on four missionary journeys. He traveled all over the known world—to Antioch, Pisidia, Galatia, Iconium, Lystra, Ephesus, Philippi, Thessalonica, Berea, Athens, Corinth, Cyprus, the island of Crete, and then eventually Rome. In addition, he trained numerous evangelists and pastors along the way. Many tried to stop him, even by stoning him in Lystra, but Paul was indefatigable (Acts 14:19).

When I was growing up, commercials for Energizer batteries featured the Energizer Bunny. The Energizer Bunny would move through various obstacles while playing a bass drum as if he were in a marching band. There would be many obstacles and many competitors, but the Energizer Bunny would outlast and outmaneuver them all. Sometimes when I read the Acts of the Apostles, I can't help but be reminded of that image. Paul just simply couldn't be stopped. He shares his heart in 2 Corinthians 11:23–28:

> Are they servants of Christ? I am a better one—I am talking like a madman—with far greater labors, far more imprisonments, with countless beatings, and often near death. Five times I received at the hands of the Jews the forty lashes less one. Three times I was beaten with rods. Once I was stoned. Three times I was shipwrecked; a night and a day I was adrift at sea; on frequent journeys, in danger from rivers, danger from

robbers, danger from my own people, danger from Gentiles, danger in the city, danger in the wilderness, danger at sea, danger from false brothers; in toil and hardship, through many a sleepless night, in hunger and thirst, often without food, in cold and exposure. And, apart from other things, there is the daily pressure on me of my anxiety for all the churches.

Paul couldn't be stopped unless he was killed—and that is exactly what the Roman emperor Nero did, probably around AD 68.

A Sanctification Manifesto

How did Paul live out this motivation? Romans 12 gives us keen insight into his strategy:

I appeal to you therefore, brothers, by the mercies of God, to present your bodies as a living sacrifice, holy and acceptable to God, which is your spiritual worship. Do not be conformed to this world, but be transformed by the renewal of your mind, that by testing you may discern what is the will of God, what is good and acceptable and perfect. (Rom. 12:1–2)

The verb that Paul uses, which is translated as "appeal," is *parakaleō*. It is a very strong Apostolic command that pictures a general speaking to his troops before they go into battle. Paul is saying: "I beseech you. I urge you." And his imperative is this: "Present your bodies as a living sacrifice, holy and acceptable to God, which is your spiritual worship" (Rom. 12:1).

The first observation that we should make about Paul's imperative is that it is a command given to believers. Some people in the modern church react negatively to any command, saying, "That's legalism!" But legalism occurs when unbiblical, self-righteous imperatives are given as if they were Scripture. It is not legalism to exhort a believer to obey what Scripture clearly commands. Commands are fundamental for understanding our role in sanctification.

The second observation we should make is what motivates Paul's command. Paul says that it is "the mercies of God" (Rom. 12:1). In other words, a proper understanding of the mercy of God in the gospel propels us to honor and obey God. Rather than motivating us to live licentiously, grace actually fuels a life lived for God. Remembering the glorious work that God has done in our lives fuels our worship. Paul never forgot that he had not always been Paul the Apostle but had once been Paul the Pharisee. His parents had sent him to Jerusalem to study under an expert in the law named Gamaliel, and Paul became his brightest student. Paul describes himself by saying, "I was advancing in Judaism beyond many of my own age among my people, so extremely zealous was I for the traditions of my fathers" (Gal. 1:14). He was the shining future of Judaism. But all that came crashing to the ground on the Damascus road.

To understand Paul's view of God's mercy, we must go back even before his Damascus road experience to an event that exposed serious cracks in his Pharisaical foundation. Paul had previously met his theological match in the early church's young servant Stephen. Stephen had taught how the Christian's worship is not confined to the temple (see Acts 7). Paul listened to this message, along with the other Jews, and they became so enraged at Stephen's proclamation of how the Lord Jesus Christ was now the center of worship that they picked up stones to kill him. They laid their tunics at Paul's feet (v. 58), and he watched as they killed that young man. That event set him off in misguided zeal. I think there was a form of covetousness and envy in his heart—he desired to know God the way that Stephen did. But instead of humbling himself and coming to Christ, he set out to persecute the church. He admits in 1 Timothy 1:13, "I was a blasphemer, persecutor, and insolent opponent." He was the one throwing people into jail. He became the chief opponent of the church. All this hate and covetousness preceded Paul's Damascus road experience.

The Damascus Road

Paul received a commission from the Jewish authorities to go to Damascus to throw Christians into jail (Acts 9:2). He was "breathing threats and murder against the disciples of the Lord" (v. 1). It was in this state that the Lord Jesus Christ Himself confronted Paul in a shining light as he neared Damascus (v. 3). The Lord said to him, using Paul's Hebrew name, "Saul, Saul, why are you persecuting me?" (v. 4). Overcome by the light and the voice, Paul fell to the ground. In what must have been stunned fear, Paul asked, "Who are you, Lord?" And Jesus replied, "I am Jesus, whom you are persecuting" (v. 5).

Jesus then told Paul to "rise" and go into the city, where he would receive further instructions (v. 6). There was just one problem: Paul had been struck blind (v. 8). He had to be led by his entourage into the city, and there he waited in blindness for three days. The Lord told Ananias through a vision to go and lay hands on Paul and pray over him (vv. 10–16). Through the prayer of Ananias, Paul regained his sight and received the indwelling Holy Spirit (vv. 17–18).

When Paul speaks of the mercy of God in his life, this is what he is referring to. Christ confronted him and changed him. If we are Christians, this is also our story. We are not born Christians. In fact, quite the opposite: we are born sinners and enemies of God (Rom. 3:23). We are born in slavery to sin (6:16–18). For us to be saved, God must intervene in our lives, as he did for Paul. Through the gospel, the Holy Spirit brings about the new birth so that we can repent and believe (John 3:1–8). No one can be born again for us or trust Christ for us. Each of us must be born again, and only the mercy and grace of God will bring this transformation about. If you are a Christian, it is because God the Holy Spirit has given you a new heart for Him (Ezek. 36:26).

This reality of God's mercy became the motivation for Paul's entire ministry. He says in 2 Corinthians 4:1, "Having this ministry by the mercy of God, we do not lose heart." For Paul, the mercy of God motivated Paul's desire to honor God. One of the great failures of modern Christianity is that we do not understand the sweetness of grace that propels us to live this life of honor. We do not look at the cross often enough. We do not remember the radical transformation of our lives often enough. As the hymn puts it, "Love so amazing, so divine, demands my soul, my life, my all."[2] That's the motivation for a life of honor. It is where Paul started, and it is where we must start.

A Complete Sacrifice

A third observation about Paul's sanctification manifesto is that he calls us to *give our lives in complete totality to the honor of God*. We are to present our bodies as living sacrifices, holy and acceptable to Him (Rom. 12:1). The language that Paul uses is reminiscent of an Old Testament sacrifice, in which someone would present a goat or a bull as an offering of worship to God. The great difference in the new covenant is that the sacrifice we give is not a goat or a bull but ourselves.

Why does Paul say "bodies" and not "souls" here? I think Paul uses the term "bodies" because he wants us to understand the complete nature of the sacrifice. At this point in history, some were teaching the gnostic idea that the soul is good while the body is bad. Since they taught that the body is evil, they argued that people could do whatever they wanted with their bodies. For them, it was only the soul that mattered. Paul obliterates this heresy in his letters: "The body is not meant for sexual immorality, but for the Lord, and the Lord for the body" (1 Cor. 6:13). He then says: "Do you not know that your body is a temple of the Holy Spirit within you, whom you have from God? You are not your own, for you were bought with a price. So glorify God in your body" (vv. 19–20).

We are to glorify God with both our bodies and our souls. We are to present all that we are as a sacrifice to God. That is why Paul emphasizes the body. He is saying that all our lives are to be sacrificed. Paul describes this sacrifice in three ways. He uses the adjectives "living," "holy," and "acceptable" (Rom. 12:1). In this Greek sentence, all three of these words modify and describe the sacrifice.

Being a living sacrifice means that our worship to God is to be perpetual. It is not a 9-to-5 job that we work during the day and take the evenings and weekends off. It is all to be lived for Him. In the Christian life, there are no off days. There are no days in which we do not have to flee temptation. There are no days in which we do not have to live in dependence on God in prayer. There are no days in which we can lay our worship aside for another. The Christian life is a constant and daily honoring of God. It is a living sacrifice.

Not only is it a living sacrifice, but it is a holy sacrifice. This means that our worship is to be dedicated completely to God. *Holy* means "separate" or "distinct." It means that we separate our worship completely to God. There are no other allegiances in the Christian life. There's no double-dipping between God and the world. How often have we seen those who honor God with their lips on a Sunday morning but deny Him by their lives the rest of the week? Peter exhorts: "As obedient children, do not be conformed to the passions of your former ignorance, but as he who called you is holy, you also be holy in all your conduct, since it is written, 'You shall be holy, for I am holy'" (1 Peter 1:14–16). This is the universal charge to Christians. We renounce our former passions and lusts. We separate ourselves from the passions and desires of the world. All of life is to be lived completely to God. Worship does not stop when we walk out the doors of our churches but continues into every sphere of our existence. When we live our lives in this way, Paul says, it is "acceptable" to God (Rom. 12:1). In other words, this is the full-orbed worship that God desires. Our lives, as living sacrifices, truly honor Him.

Paul sums all this up by saying that this "is your spiritual worship" (Rom. 12:1). The word that is translated as "spiritual" is the Greek word *logikos*. In that word, we see a semblance of the English word *logic*. The word means "rational" or "logical." Paul's point is that when we understand the mercy of God in our lives, this life of complete worship to God is the only rational and logical course of action. When we understand the depths from which Christ saved us, then serving Him in this way is the logical response. Iain Murray describes this mindset in D. Martyn Lloyd-Jones regarding his calling into ministry. Further, his view of preaching was such that to talk of "sacrifice" in relation to that work was virtually absurd:

> There could be no higher privilege than that of being a messenger of the God who has pledged his help and presence to those whom he sends. When, as happened at times, people referred in admiring terms to [Lloyd-Jones'] self-denial in entering the ministry, he repudiated the intended compliment completely. "I gave up nothing," he said on one such occasion, "I received everything. I count it the highest honour that God can confer on any man to call him to be a herald of the gospel."[3]

Clearly, for Lloyd-Jones, leaving the luxurious life of medicine in London for pastoral ministry in Wales was the logical conclusion to his understanding of God's mercy. That is the exact idea that Paul is getting across to us in Romans 12:1.

Where to Begin

How do we do this practically? The Apostle is quick to give specific instructions: "Do not be conformed to this world, but be transformed by the renewal of your mind" (Rom. 12:2). This is a very simple statement—a prohibition followed by a command. A negative and a positive. This is how we are to live our lives completely for Christ's honor.

First, we must look at the negative: "Do not be conformed to this world." Paul uses an interesting word here for "world." He does not use the word *kosmos*, which John uses, for example, in John 3:16. It is the word *aiōn*, which is sometimes translated "age." Paul, along with many other Jews, understood our current "age" to be contrasted with "the one to come," which will be ushered in when our Lord establishes the new heavens and new earth (Eph. 1:21). Paul uses the same word in Galatians 1:4 when he says that Christ "gave himself for our sins to deliver us from the present evil age." This is the idea that he is communicating. He is talking about renouncing the evil practices and thinking that characterize this period before our Lord's return.

Paul's prohibition is against being "conformed to" this age (Rom. 12:2). J.B. Phillips famously captured the idea when he paraphrased the statement, "Don't let the world around you squeeze you into its own mold."[4] What does this mean in our current cultural context? The predominating worldview is the idolatry of radical self-expression. Satan's deception in the modern age has been to convince people to worship their own feelings. There must be no boundaries that limit modern man's self-expression. Satan has gone so far as to even deceive people on the most basic, foundational level: their God-given gender. The desires of the flesh enslave and dominate to the degree that the sinner is mastered by them and succumbs to them (6:16). And Satan's deception has been to insist that every fleshly desire be given free rein. That is why the world today is a world of radical self-expression.

But it is not so with the Christian. Paul describes Christians as "having been set free from sin [and] become slaves of righteousness" (Rom. 6:18). Paul states his own position in relation to the world when he says that "the world has been crucified to me, and I to the world" (Gal. 6:14). The old man, whom we once were in Adam, chasing after the world, has died (Rom. 6:5). We are now new men and women in Christ (v. 8). We have already crucified the old man, and with it its desires for the things of the world. Therefore, we do not allow ourselves to be conformed to its image.

Second, the positive command is, "Be transformed by the renewal of your mind" (12:2). The Greek word translated as "transformed" is *metamorphousthe*. We can see the root of our English word *metamorphosis*. But where does Paul say that this metamorphosis is to take place? True transformation must begin in the mind. The Holy Spirit sanctifies our minds with the truth (John 17:17). Jesus said, "You will know the truth, and the truth will set you free" (John 8:32). We are to put as much of God's truth into our minds as we can, so that we are transformed into Christ's likeness (Titus 1:1).

It is in this area that so much of modern Christianity has failed. Instead of teaching believers the deep things of God, many churches have found that it is much easier to babysit them. A steady diet of entertainment and practical-living instruction will fill a building, but it will not fill the mind with truth. And if the mind is not filled with truth, then transformation cannot take place. Paul's constant exhortation is to "set your minds on things that are above, not on things that are on earth" (Col. 3:2).

How to Renew the Mind

If we are going to be successful in living for the honor of God, we must put more of God's truth in our minds than we do the world's falsehood. That is tantamount to Paul's command: Renew your mind with holy *truth*. This is a word that we desperately need to hear. Many believers are more influenced by social media than they are by the book of Romans. And we must change that and fill our minds with biblical truth. How do we do that? Here are eight practical ways:

1. View the world through a Psalm 19 lens. This means that we understand creation and everything that we experience in nature as pointing us to the glory of God. Every sunrise, mountain peak, and starry evening declares the glory of our Creator. When we see the beauty in creation, we ought to meditate on what that tells us about the character of God.

2. Read or listen to the Bible daily. We have so many opportunities today to read and study the Word of God. Most modern Christians own multiple Bibles, and the Word of God is at our fingertips. This may surprise some people, but it takes only around twenty minutes a day to read through the entire Bible in a year. As we take in the Word of God daily, it radically renews our minds.

3. Memorize Scripture. Psalm 119:11 says, "I have stored up your word in my heart, that I might not sin against you." A Scripture-stored mind is a source of truth that we can constantly go back to again and again, just as Jesus did during His temptation. When we are intentionally focused on hardwiring our minds with Scripture, it becomes even more a part of us.

4. Meditate on Scripture. Meditating on Scripture involves rolling it over in our minds and asking some questions. What does this passage teach about God? What does it say about us? What does it say about how we are to live? What does it mean? It's amazing that we could potentially take one verse of Scripture and meditate on it for the rest of our lives and still not exhaust its depth—such is the richness of Scripture. Meditation brings the Word of God from the mind into our affections. David observes that the godly man meditates on the Word of God day and night (Ps. 1).

5. Listen to expository preaching. There is a reason that Paul told Timothy to "preach the word ... in season and out of season" (2 Tim. 4:2). The Word of God preached confronts us and renews our minds in new ways. The Holy Spirit uses the Word of God to change us in ways that we were not expecting. As Paul told the Corinthians, his message came "in demonstration of the Spirit and of power" (1 Cor. 2:4). The Word of God, through preaching, comes to us in the power of the Holy Spirit.

6. Sing great hymns of the faith. Over and over in the New Testament, we are exhorted to sing "psalms and hymns and spiritual songs" (Eph. 5:19; Col. 3:16). We learn our theology through singing. Singing is a critical way for our minds to be renewed with truth. My family loves to sing the Doxology together before dinner. Our three-year-old son now knows it so well that he desires to lead in the singing. I love this because it means that a doxological theology is already ingrained deep into his mind.

7. Pray without ceasing. We are instructed to live our lives in constant prayer to God (Eph. 6:18; 1 Thess. 5:17). We strive to live in continual communion with our Lord. If we are praying throughout our day, then our minds will be set on spiritual things rather than carnal things. We will be focused on God's will being done in our lives and not our own.

8. Develop a biblical worldview. When we put the previous seven principles together, we will quickly begin to develop a biblical worldview—a view of the world that is informed and controlled by the Word of God. This means that we do not see the world neutrally but rather see it with certain presuppositional truths that anchor our view of God, the world, people, politics, ethics, and everything else under the sun. We watch everything, read everything, and look at everything with the mind of Christ. Paul explains in 2 Corinthians 10:5, "We destroy arguments and every lofty opinion raised against the knowledge of God, and take every thought captive to obey Christ." That is the idea. God's truth must be hardwired into our souls such that we filter everything we encounter through the truth. Those "arguments" and "lofty opinions" that contradict the truth are cast down. We can further develop a biblical worldview by reading sound Christian literature. This has helped me immensely over the years. Obviously, nothing should replace our study of Scripture, but reading sound Christian literature helps us develop a biblical worldview.

Loving the Perfect Will of God

When we have done these things, by the power of the Holy Spirit, our minds will be renewed and our affections will change. We will find that we love doing the will of God. In our experience of renewing our minds, we will come to know "what is the will of God, what is good and acceptable and perfect" (Rom. 12:2). Paul is referencing not God's secret will of decree here but His preceptive will as revealed in His Word. As we live out the Word of God and think the Word of God, we come to understand and affirm its goodness.

The three adjectives "good," "acceptable," and "perfect" are ways that Paul is describing the will of God. He exhorts us that by living through the renewing of the mind, we see as a result that the will of God is good, acceptable, and perfect. This really is the mindset of the believer—that God's will is proved to be good to us. It is proved to be acceptable to us. It is proved to be perfect to us. Probably one of the places where we see this most is Psalm 119. Over and over again, the psalmist declares that the will of the Lord, the commandments of the Lord, the law of the Lord is good, right, and perfect.

David proclaims in Psalm 19:7, "The law of the LORD is perfect, reviving the soul; the testimony of the LORD is sure, making wise the simple." He asserts in Psalm 19:8, "The precepts of the LORD are right, rejoicing the heart." In Psalm 119:35, the psalmist exclaims, "Lead me in the path of your commandments, for I delight in it." In other words, the life of honor is vindicated as good in our own lives. We find that we love it and enjoy it. We begin to wonder: "How could I have ever pursued any other course of action? How could I have ever lived any other way?" We begin to look at people who live their lives contrary to the Word of God and have pity on them. We pray for them. We realize how thankful we are to be living the life of honor. It is not lost on us that God has had mercy on us.

And that leads us full circle. This is why Paul could say in Philippians 1:21 that "to live is Christ, and to die is gain." Living Christ's life through the renewing of the mind and loving the will of God is the best life that Paul could possibly live.

Conclusion

When you live for God's honor, your life will matter for eternity. Your life will count for the only thing that truly counts forever. Moreover, you will become a person of transcendence. With your gaze set on Christ, you will fear no man. In every situation, you will see past it and through it to our triune God, who is above it.

This is the type of Christian that the church desperately needs today. This is the type of Christian that the world needs today— Christians whose hearts burn with a passion for God's name to be honored at whatever the cost.

Notes

Introduction

1   Wilfred M. McClay, *Land of Hope: An Invitation to the Great American Story* (New York: Encounter, 2019), 89.

2   *Breathtaking: K2—The World's Most Dangerous Mountain*, Eddie Bauer Presents (documentary), YouTube, 2020, https://www.youtube.com/watch?v=cvFt2Xcuois.

3   See article in *Tabletalk* magazine where I recount more of my experience of coming to understand the reality of living *coram Deo*. Grant R. Castleberry, "Time and Vocation," *Tabletalk*, September 2020.

4   Sinclair Ferguson, "Preaching and Preachers" (lecture, Martyn Lloyd-Jones Memorial Lectures, London Seminary, October 25, 2019), https://pastorsacademy.podbean.com/e/martyn-lloyd-jones-memorial-lecture-2019/.

5   Martyn Lloyd-Jones, *Revival* (Westchester, Ill.: Crossway, 1987), 37.

6   Lloyd-Jones, 37–38.

Chapter 1

1   Duncan Hamilton, *For the Glory: Eric Liddell's Journey from Olympic Champion to Modern Martyr* (New York: Penguin, 2016), 102–4.

2   Hamilton, 103.

Chapter 2

1   I was first exposed to this idea of God's seeking His own pleasure on a mission trip in high school when a missionary handed me John Piper's *The Pleasures of God* on the plane. It was paradigm-shaping for me. John Piper, *The Pleasures of God: Meditations on God's Delight in Being God*, rev. and expanded ed. (Sisters, Ore.: Multnomah, 2000).

2   *Works of Jonathan Edwards*, vol. 8, *Ethical Writings*, ed. Paul Ramsey (New Haven, Conn.: Yale University Press, 1989), 420.

3   Edwards, 421.
4   Edwards, 421.
5   Edwards, 421.
6   Edwards, 422.
7   Edwards, 424.
8   Piper, *Pleasures of God*, 14.
9   John Frame writes: "The ground is 'holy' not because there is something special or dangerous about the ground as such, but because Yahweh is there, the supremely Holy One. God's messenger is to stand back, to remove his shoes in respect. He is afraid to look at the face of God." John M. Frame, *Systematic Theology: An Introduction to Christian Belief* (Phillipsburg, N.J.: P&R, 2013), 277.
10 Stephen Charnock, *The Existence and Attributes of God* (repr., Grand Rapids, Mich.: Baker, 2000), 50.

Chapter 3

1   John Calvin, *Institutes of the Christian Religion*, trans. Robert White (1541; repr., Edinburgh, Scotland: Banner of Truth, 2014), 1.
2   D. Martyn Lloyd-Jones, "Blinded by Sin," sermon 5230, MLJ Trust, n.d., https://www.mljtrust.org/sermons-online/psalms-8-3-4/blinded-by-sin-2/.
3   Harold L. Senkbeil, *The Care of Souls: Cultivating a Pastor's Heart* (Bellingham, Wash.: Lexham, 2019), 138–39.
4   David Seal, "Shame," in *The Lexham Bible Dictionary*, ed. John D. Barry et al. (Bellingham, Wash.: Lexham, 2016).
5   Aubrey Sequeira, Radius International: Clear Gospel. True Gospel, Twitter, March 1, 2023, https://twitter.com/i/status/1630251639188889601.

Chapter 4

1   Iain Murray included this statement on the cover flap of his outstanding book *Heroes*. Iain H. Murray, *Heroes* (Edinburgh, Scotland: Banner of Truth, 2008).

Chapter 5

1   Anselm of Canterbury, *The Major Works including Monologion, Proslogion, and Why God Became Man*, Oxford World's Classics (Oxford, England: Oxford University Press, 1998), 283.

2   Anselm of Canterbury, 283.

3   Anselm of Canterbury, 286.

4   Leon Morris, *The Gospel according to John*, Rev. ed. New International Commentary on the New Testament (Grand Rapids, Mich.: Eerdmans, 1995), 665.

Chapter 6

1   This was the explanation of the Pentecostal blessing by R.C. Sproul; it was formative in my framework of understanding the baptism of the Holy Spirit. R.C. Sproul, "Undervaluing Pentecost" (Strange Fire Conference, Sun Valley, Calif.: Grace to You, 2013), https://www.youtube.com/watch?v=f37jFQlb6aQ.

Chapter 7

1   Iain Murray gives us fascinating insight into how Lloyd-Jones counseled. He often met counselees in his vestry after the morning service—his counseling ministry was dynamically connected to his pulpit ministry. Iain H. Murray, *D. Martyn Lloyd-Jones*, vol. 2, *The Fight of Faith: 1939–1981* (Edinburgh, Scotland: Banner of Truth, 1990), 403.

2   For a thorough explanation of Bible-centered worship, see chapters 5 and 6 of Dr. Terry Johnson's book on worship. Terry L. Johnson, *Worshipping with Calvin: Recovering the Historic Ministry and Worship of Reformed Protestantism* (Grand Rapids, Mich.: EP, 2014), 80–221.

3   Martyn Lloyd-Jones, *Revival* (Westchester, Ill.: Crossway, 1987), 103.

4   Sinclair B. Ferguson, *Devoted to God's Church: Core Values for Christian Fellowship* (Edinburgh, Scotland: Banner of Truth, 2020), 159–60.

5   Dr. Sproul writes: "Only once in sacred Scripture is an attribute of God elevated to the third degree. Only once is a characteristic of God mentioned three times in succession. The Bible says that God is holy, holy, holy. Not that He is merely holy, or even holy, holy. He is holy, holy, holy. The Bible never says that God is love, love, love; or mercy, mercy, mercy; or wrath, wrath, wrath; or justice, justice, justice. It does say that He is holy, holy, holy, that the whole earth is full of His glory." R.C. Sproul, *The Holiness of God* (Wheaton, Ill.: Tyndale House, 1985), 25.

Chapter 8

1   John Piper, *Let the Nations Be Glad! The Supremacy of God in Missions* (Grand Rapids, Mich.: Baker, 1993), 11.
2   Piper, 15.
3   Iain H. Murray, *Jonathan Edwards: A New Biography* (Edinburgh, Scotland: Banner of Truth, 1987), 302.
4   Murray, 302.
5   Murray, 305.

Chapter 9

1   See Michael Reeves, "John Bunyan: The Minister's Fear of God" (UK Ministers' Conference, Yarnfield Park, Staffordshire, England: Banner of Truth, 2018), https://youtu.be/r4VPKXrtyFQ.

Chapter 10

1   Herman Bavinck, *Reformed Dogmatics*, vol. 3, *Sin and Salvation in Christ*, ed. John Bolt, trans. John Vriend (Grand Rapids, Mich.: Baker Academic, 2006), 528.
2   Isaac Watts, "When I Survey the Wondrous Cross" (1707).
3   Iain H. Murray, *D. Martyn Lloyd-Jones*, vol. 1, *The First Forty Years: 1899–1939* (Edinburgh, Scotland: Banner of Truth, 1982), 150–51.
4   J.B. Phillips, trans., *The New Testament in Modern English* (New York: Macmillan, 1964), 341.

Bibliography

Anselm of Canterbury. *The Major Works Including Monologion, Proslogion, and Why God Became Man*. Oxford World's Classics. Oxford, England: Oxford University Press, 1998.

Bavinck, Herman. *Reformed Dogmatics*. Vol. 3, *Sin and Salvation in Christ*. Edited by John Bolt. Translated by John Vriend. Grand Rapids, Mich.: Baker Academic, 2006.

Breathtaking: K2—The World's Most Dangerous Mountain. Eddie Bauer Presents (documentary). YouTube, 2020. https://www.youtube.com/watch?v=cvFt2Xcuois.

Calvin, John. *Institutes of the Christian Religion*. Translated by Robert White. 1541. Reprint, Edinburgh, Scotland: Banner of Truth, 2014.

Castleberry, Grant R. "Time and Vocation." *Tabletalk*, September 2020.

Charnock, Stephen. *The Existence and Attributes of God*. Reprint, Grand Rapids, Mich.: Baker, 2000.

Edwards, Jonathan. *Works of Jonathan Edwards*. Vol. 8, *Ethical Writings*. Edited by Paul Ramsey. New Haven, Conn.: Yale University Press, 1989.

Ferguson, Sinclair B. *Devoted to God's Church: Core Values for Christian Fellowship*. Edinburgh, Scotland; Carlisle, PA: Banner of Truth, 2020.

———. "Preaching and Preachers." Lecture presented at the Martyn Lloyd-Jones Memorial Lectures, London Seminary, October 25, 2019. https://pastorsacademy.podbean.com/e/martyn-lloyd-jones-memorial-lecture-2019/.

Frame, John M. *Systematic Theology: An Introduction to Christian Belief*. Phillipsburg, N.J.: P&R, 2013.

Hamilton, Duncan. *For the Glory: Eric Liddell's Journey from Olympic Champion to Modern Martyr*. New York: Penguin, 2016.

Johnson, Terry L. *Worshipping with Calvin: Recovering the Historic Ministry and Worship of Reformed Protestantism*. Grand Rapids, Mich.: EP, 2014.

Lloyd-Jones, D. Martyn. "Blinded by Sin." Sermon 5230. MLJ Trust, n.d. https://www.mljtrust.org/sermons-online/psalms-8-3-4/blinded-by-sin-2/.

———. *Revival*. Westchester, Ill.: Crossway, 1987.

McClay, Wilfred M. *Land of Hope: An Invitation to the Great American Story*. New York: Encounter, 2019.

Morris, Leon. *The Gospel according to John*. Rev. ed. New International Commentary on the New Testament. Grand Rapids, Mich.: Eerdmans, 1995.

Murray, Iain H. *D. Martyn Lloyd-Jones*. Vol. 1, *The First Forty Years: 1899–1939*. Edinburgh, Scotland: Banner of Truth, 1982.

———. *D. Martyn Lloyd-Jones*. Vol. 2, *The Fight of Faith: 1939–1981*. Edinburgh, Scotland: Banner of Truth, 1990.

———. *Heroes*. Edinburgh, Scotland: Banner of Truth, 2008.

———. *Jonathan Edwards: A New Biography*. Edinburgh, Scotland: Banner of Truth, 1987.

Phillips, J.B., trans. *The New Testament in Modern English*. New York: Macmillan, 1964.

Piper, John. *Let the Nations Be Glad! The Supremacy of God in Missions*. Grand Rapids, Mich.: Baker, 1993.

———. *The Pleasures of God: Meditations on God's Delight in Being God*. Rev. and expanded ed. Sisters, Ore.: Multnomah, 2000.

Reeves, Michael. "John Bunyan: The Minister's Fear of God." UK Ministers' Conference, Yarnfield Park, Staffordshire, England: Banner of Truth, 2018. https://youtu.be/r4VPKXrtyFQ.

Senkbeil, Harold L. *The Care of Souls: Cultivating a Pastor's Heart*. Bellingham, Wash.: Lexham, 2019.

Sequeira, Aubrey. Radius International: Clear Gospel. True Gospel. Twitter, March 1, 2023. https://twitter.com/i/status/1630251639188889601.

Sproul, R.C. *The Holiness of God*. Wheaton, Ill.: Tyndale House, 1985.

———. "Undervaluing Pentecost." Strange Fire Conference, Sun Valley, Calif.: Grace to You, 2013. https://www.youtube.com/watch?v=f37jFQlb6aQ.

Scripture Index

About the Author

Grant R. Castleberry (M.Div. and Th.M., The Southern Baptist Theological Seminary, Louisville, Ky.) is a pastor in Raleigh, N.C., and president and Bible teacher of Unashamed Truth Ministries. He and his wife, GraceAnna, have five children.